GREAT LEGAL
DISASTERS

GREAT LEGAL DISASTERS

Stephen Tumim

Illustrations by Bernard Cookson

"No, no!" said the Queen. "Sentence first –
verdict afterwards."

GUILD PUBLISHING
London

This edition published in 1985 by
Book Club Associates by arrangement
with Arthur Barker Limited

Photoset, printed and bound
in Great Britain by
Redwood Burn Limited
Trowbridge, Wiltshire

Contents

A judge . . . is not to play at marbles, or chuck farthing in the piazza.

Preface

'A judge', said Doctor Johnson, 'may be a farmer but he is not to geld his own pigs. A judge may play a little at cards for his own amusement, but he is not to play at marbles, or chuck farthing in the piazza.' Fearful of offence, I have stayed clear of recent disasters, and played safe with the past.

Disaster at law (despite Lord Kenyon's spot of trouble with the vase) does not usually strike with a swoosh or a thud but with a few ill-chosen words. I have kept, as far as I can, to the words actually spoken at the time and to the particular moment of calamity. Where the whole trial was a disaster, or the disaster crept up in stages, the story lengthens and the mood varies.

Disaster at law usually ends in tears, even if it is disaster of the wig-falls-off variety. There is too much at stake. When it is an example of that system of official brutality heightened by occasional not very discriminate pardon, which lingered unhappily on in our criminal system until well into the nineteenth century, it becomes unreadable. In 1831 a boy of nine was publicly hanged in Chelmsford for arson. This was no exceptional case. I have, I hope, avoided the unreadable, but it is there, in the unavoidable background.

I have not sought to avoid the most famous disasters, as even the learned sometimes forget the words. As Sellar or Yeatman tells us : 'History is not what you thought. It is what you can remember.'

I make my bow to many kind lawyers who have, one way or another, put me in mind of disaster, and to friends who have drawn my attention to cases I would otherwise have omitted, in particular (in the latter category) to Michael Birks, Nigel Curtis-Raleigh, Simon Levene, Brian Masters and John Vaizey. For the additional disaster of failing to get it right, I alone am responsible.

1. Rough Justice and a Thirsty Jury 1603 – 1688

The curtain rises with two great men losing their tempers in court, drawing from the judge a memorably soothing remark.

SIR WALTER RALEIGH: If My Lord Cobham be a Traitor, what is that to me?

SIR EDWARD COKE, ATTORNEY-GENERAL: All that he did was by thy instigation, thou viper; for I 'thou' thee, thou traitor.

RALEIGH: It becometh not a man of quality and virtue to call me so: but I take comfort in it, it is all you can do.

COKE: Have I angered you?

RALEIGH: I am in no case to be angry.

LORD CHIEF-JUSTICE POPHAM: Sir Walter Raleigh, Mr Attorney speaketh out of the zeal of his duty, for the service of the King, and you for your life; be valiant on both sides.

To 'tutoyer', to call a gentleman 'thou' instead of you, was in 1603 the depth of offensiveness, a true four-letter word, and its use was a shock to Raleigh. Once he had recovered, he had no difficulty in treating the Attorney-General's abuse with contempt.

COKE: Thou art the most vile and execrable traitor that ever lived.

RALEIGH: You speak indiscreetly, barbarously and uncivilly.

COKE: I want words sufficient to express thy viperous treasons.

RALEIGH: I think you want words indeed, for you have

1

spoken one thing half a dozen times.

COKE: Thou art an odious fellow, thy name is hateful to all the realm of England for thy pride.

RALEIGH: It will go near to prove a measuring cast between you and me, Mr Attorney.

Sir Walter Raleigh was convicted of treason by the jury (probably wrongly on the evidence produced), and sentenced to the customary horrid death.

'The judgment of this court is, that you shall be had from hence to the place whence you came, there to remain, until the day of execution; and from thence you shall be drawn upon a hurdle through the open streets to the place of execution, there to be hanged and cut down alive, and your body shall be opened, your heart and bowels plucked out, and your privy members cut off, and thrown into the fire before your eyes; then your head to be stricken off from your body, and your body shall be divided into four quarters, to be disposed of at the King's pleasure: and God have mercy upon your soul.'

These disasters he partially avoided. Execution of the sentence was deferred. For thirteen years he remained a prisoner in the Tower, where he engaged in family life, philosophy, scientific experiments and literature, and in tutoring the Prince of Wales. In 1616 he was allowed out to lead an expedition to the Orinoco in pursuit of gold. It was a complete failure and on his return in 1618 he was beheaded in pursuance of part of the old sentence of 1603. The Attorney-General, who had so rancorously taunted him at his trial, died in 1638 in honourable retirement, the revered champion of the independence of the judges and a founding father of our modern legal system.

Although rough justice was a regular hazard for the political climber, it also befell less worldly persons. In 1660 John Bunyan was charged at quarter sessions as 'a person who devilishly and perniciously abstained from coming to church to hear divine service, and a common upholder of unlawful meetings and conventicles, to the great disturbance and distraction of the good subjects of this realm'.

He replied: 'Show me the place in the Epistles where the Common Prayer Book is written, or one text of scripture that commands me to read it, and I will use it. But yet, notwithstanding, they that have a mind to use it, they have their liberty; that is, I would not keep them from it. But, for our own parts, we can pray to God without it. Blessed be His name.'

The court, perhaps further disturbed and distracted, promptly and wrongly took this address as a plea of guilty, and proceeded to pronounce a sentence unjustified by any extant law. 'You must be had back to prison, and there lie for three months following; and at three months' end, if you do not submit to go to church to hear divine service, and leave your preaching, you must be banished the realm. And if, after such a day as shall be appointed you to be gone, you shall be found in this realm, or be found to come over again without special licence from the King, you must stretch by the neck for it; I tell you plainly.'

Bunyan refused to give surety to abstain from preaching. He was imprisoned. Mrs Bunyan applied to the House of Lords for his release, and was referred to the judges at the next assizes. She appeared before Sir Matthew Hale and Mr Justice Twisden.

MRS BUNYAN: The Lords told me that releasement was committed to you, and you give me neither releasement nor relief. My husband is unlawfully in prison, and you are bound to discharge him.

TWISDEN: He has been lawfully convicted.

MRS BUNYAN: It is false, for when they said: 'Do you confess the indictment?' he answered, at the meetings where he preached, they had God's presence among them.

TWISDEN: Will your husband leave preaching? If he will do so, then send for him.

MRS BUNYAN: My Lord, he dares not leave off preaching as long as he can speak. But, good My Lords, consider that we have four small children, one of them blind, and that they have nothing to live upon, while their father is in prison, but the charity of Christian people. I myself 'smayed at the news when my husband was apprehended, and being but young, and unaccustomed to such things, fell in labour; and, continuing it for eight days, was delivered of a dead child.

HALE: Alas, poor woman.

TWISDEN: Poverty is your cloak, for I hear your husband is better maintained by running up and down a-preaching than by following his calling.

HALE: What is his calling?

MRS BUNYAN: A tinker, please you, My Lord; and because he is a tinker, and a poor man, therefore he is despised, and cannot have justice.

HALE: I am truly sorry we can do you no good. Sitting here, we can only act as the law gives us warrant; and we have no power to reverse the sentence, although it may be erroneous.

John Bunyan remained in prison for some twelve years until he was released under Charles II's Declaration of Indulgence. *The Pilgrim's Progress* was not written during this period of enforced leisure, but during a later imprisonment. In the trial of Faithful and Christian he caught the judicial tone of Mrs Bunyan's forlorn attempt to appeal.

In the early seventeenth century the harrassing of witches was a popular pursuit. But by the reign of Charles II greater scepticism and the Royal Society were emerging and trials for witchcraft were becoming rare in England, although a spate was still to sully New England. The trial of two widows at Bury St Edmunds in 1665 was peculiar not only for its late date, but for the bland disregard of common sense with which it was conducted. The judge, the conductor, was the celebrated Sir Matthew Hale who a few years earlier had made useless, if comforting, sounds to Mrs Bunyan.

Rose Callender and Amy Duny were tried on thirteen indictments for bewitching their neighbours, including the bewitching of the children of four families. None of these children gave evidence. Elizabeth Durent had died. William Durent was too young. Jane Bocking and Deborah Pacy were said to be too bewitched to come. Ann Durent, Susan Chandler and Elizabeth Pacy all came to give evidence, but when they arrived at the court-house each fell into 'a strange and violent fit, shrieking out in a most sad manner', and was struck dumb until the case was over. The court had to make do with the parents as witnesses.

Mrs Durent recounted how she had left young William with Amy Duny while she went shopping, had given Amy a penny for her trouble and had forbidden her to suckle the child, because, as she told the jury, Amy had long had the reputation of being a witch. But on her return, Amy said William had been so hungry she had been obliged to suckle him. There were 'high expressions' between the two women, and that night William fell into a faint. Mrs Durent consulted Dr Jacob of Yarmouth, a specialist in bewitched children. He advised her to hang up William's blanket in the chimney-corner all day, and when she came to put William to bed, if she found anything in the blanket, to throw it into the fire. Mrs Durent followed these instructions and when she took down the blanket out of it fell a great toad. As soon as it was in the fire it made a great and horrible noise, and after a space there was a flashing in the fire like gunpowder, making a noise like the discharge of a pistol, and thereupon the toad was no more seen or heard.

Next day Mrs Durent went to confront Amy, who was 'sitting all alone in her house in her smock without any fire'. Her face and legs and thighs were scorched and she was in a most lamentable condition. 'This deponent seemed much to wonder, and asked the said Amy how she came into that sad condition? And the said Amy replied, she might thank her for it, for that this deponent was the cause of it, but that she should live to see some of her children dead, and she upon crutches. And this deponent further saith, that after the burning of the said toad, her child recovered, and was well again, and was living at the time of the assizes.'

Then Elizabeth, Mrs Durent's ten-year-old, fell ill. Mrs Durent went to the apothecary for medicine. When she returned she found Amy in her house. Amy told her she had given Elizabeth some water. Mrs Durent pushed Amy out with more 'high expressions'. Amy said: 'You need not be so angry, for your child will not live long.' Elizabeth died two days later, and Mrs Durent was overcome by lameness. 'After she had gone upon crutches for upwards of three years, and went upon them at the time of the assizes in the court when she gave her evidence, and upon the jury's bringing in their verdict, by which the said Amy Duny was found guilty, to the great admiration of all persons, the said Dorothy Durent was restored to the use of her limbs, and went home without making use of her crutches.'

But the dramatic extras at the trial were not limited to the miracle of the crutches or to the shrieks of the non-witnesses. Elizabeth Pacy, aged eleven, was brought into court and deposited. She affected a deep sleep, and would move no part of her body; she laid her head, covered by her apron, on the bar of the court and lay there a good long time. Finally, by the direction of the judge, Amy Duny was brought to Elizabeth Pacy, and touched the girl's hand. 'Whereupon the child without so much as seeing her, for her eyes were closed all the while, suddenly leaped up, and catched Amy Duny by the hand, and afterwards by the face; and with her nails scratched her till blood came, and would by no means leave her till she

. . . and there she lay a good long time.

was taken from her, and afterwards the child would still be pressing towards her, and making signs of anger conceived against her.'

The oral evidence about the Pacy girls was given by their father, Samuel Pacy, a sober merchant from Lowestoft, and their aunt, Margaret Arnold, from Yarmouth. Mr Pacy told the court that Deborah had become lame, and one sunny day she was carried outside to where she could enjoy a nice view of the sea. Amy Duny came to buy herrings from Mr Pacy. She was refused. She came back several times, got no herrings, and went off grumbling. At this moment Deborah 'was taken with most violent fits, feeling most extreme pains in her stomach, like the pricking of pins, and shrieking out in a most dreadful manner like unto a whelp; and not like unto a sensible creature'. Mr Pacy called in Dr Feavor, but as that learned man was unable to diagnose what was wrong, Mr Pacy knew it must be witchcraft. Mr Pacy was a man of substance and he complained. Amy was promptly set in the stocks. While she sat there two local women asked her what was wrong with Deborah. Amy replied that when her children had been ill, she had forced them to eat and Deborah's mouth should be topped in the same way. Three days later the older Pacy daughter, Elizabeth, fell into fits. Both children were apparently somewhat relieved by forced feeding, as Amy had indicated, but they continued to have fits and nightmares, in which they called out the names of Amy and of Rose Callender, the other defendant. At this stage in his evidence, Mr Pacy began to speak more in the style of Mrs Durent. 'They would fall', he said, 'into swoonings, and upon the recovery to their speech they would cough extremely, and bring up much phlegm, and with the same crooked pins, and one time a twopenny nail with a very broad head ... commonly at the end of every fit they would cast up a pin, and sometimes they would have four or five fits in one day.' Mr Pacy produced to the court a packet of pins and the nail.

The girls were then sent for a change of air to Yarmouth, to their aunt, Mrs Arnold, who carried on the story. At the start

8

she had not believed the children. She took their dresses, and found them full of pins. She sewed up the dresses, so that there was no need to pin them, and less room for concealment. But the girls continued to produce pins, to throw fits, and to blame Amy and Rose. Mrs Arnold was puzzled and let the children know it. A plague of invisible mice promptly appeared to them. One of the children 'snapped one with the tongs and threw it in the fire, and it screached out like a rat'. Then Deborah came running into the house, saying a bee had flown into her face trying to put a nail into her mouth, and she threw a fit and vomited up another twopenny nail with a broad head. Elizabeth cried out that there was a mouse under the table. She crept after it, and threw into the fire something Mrs Arnold could not see. There was a flash like gunpowder. Elizabeth ran round the house, put something in her apron and threw it on the fire. Again Mrs Arnold did not see it. Elizabeth said it was a duck. Mrs Arnold came reluctantly to accept that the children were bewitched. It must have been a very uncomfortable visit for the poor aunt.

The prosecution case ended with Mrs Bocking and Mrs Chandler giving similar evidence about their own daughters, fits and pin-vomiting to the fore. Then came a most unusual scene. 'Divers known persons' attending the assize, country gentlemen and serjeants-at-law, did not think much of the evidence, and the judge decided to allow a more rational test than that previously tried out on Elizabeth Pacy. One of the bewitched girls had an apron put over her face. She was touched by Amy. She shrieked. She was touched by someone else. She shrieked again. 'Whereupon the gentlemen returned, openly protesting, that they did believe the whole transaction of this business was a mere imposture. This put the court and all persons into a stand.'

But not for long. The judge could have stopped the case and discharged the defendants. Instead, 'Dr Brown of Norwich, a person of great knowledge, who was in court, was invited to give his opinion'. If Dr Brown's evidence was the first psychiatric evidence to be given in the courts, it was not a happy start, for he upheld the business of bewitching, learnedly comparing the case in question with recent discoveries of witchcraft in Denmark. He claimed the strange fits, the needles and nails, were caused by 'the devil, co-operating with the malice of these which we term witches, at whose instance he doth these villanies'.

When Dr Brown was done, witnesses gave more evidence of sinister conduct by Amy and Rose, mostly unconnected with the charges on which they stood trial. After trouble with Amy, it was evident that chimneys fell, geese and pigs died, fish slid from boats back into the sea.

Sir Matthew Hale summed up the case with the most remarkable brevity. His opening line fills a modern judge with envy. 'He told them that he would not repeat the evidence unto them, lest by so doing he should wrong the evidence on the one side or on the other. Only this acquainted them, that they had two things to enquire after. First, whether or no these children were bewitched? Secondly, whether the prisoners at the bar were guilty of it? That there were such creatures as witches he made no doubt at all; for first, the scriptures had affirmed so much. Secondly the wisdom of all nations had provided laws against such persons, which is an argument of their confidence in such a crime. . . .'

He made no mention of the tests on the girls, nor did he raise the possibility that the children might have been concocting a story. Half an hour later the jury returned with verdicts of guilty on each charge. Next morning the three children, Ann Durent, Susan Chandler and Elizabeth Pacy, all recovered their tongues and senses. Their parents hurried them to the judge's lodgings, and were directed to take them to court, where Susan and Elizabeth, Ann being too frightened still, said they had been bewitched as their parents had stated.

It was a Friday. Sir Matthew sentenced Amy and Rose to be hanged on the Monday. He went off that afternoon to Cambridge to prepare for the next assize and applied himself over the weekend to writing a 'Meditation concerning the mercy of God in preserving us from the malice and power of Evil

10

Angels', in which he referred with some complacency to the trial. Some years after the hanging of Amy and Rose, Dr Brown was knighted, and passed down to posterity as Sir Thomas Browne, the author of the noblest meditation in English.

The acquittal of the Seven Bishops in 1688, who had petitioned James II to stay within the Church of England and to honour his coronation oath, and were charged with sedition, set the church bells ringing and brought down the House of Stuart.

Late in the previous evening the jury had been sent out to consider their verdict. The Lord Chief Justice had allowed them some wine before they went. Then the jury bailiff had been sworn in accordance with law: 'You shall well and truly keep every person sworn in this jury in some private and convenient room without meat, drink, fire, candle or lodging . . . .' Luckily for them it was midsummer. The court did not sit until ten in the morning.

They were locked up in the dark. All night solicitors for the defence lurked outside to ensure that the ushers, servants of the Crown, did not bribe the jurors with food or drink. At four in the morning basins of water were sent in so that the jury might wash.

They drank the lot.

The jury list had been anxiously checked by the King himself, and the jury consisted of well-to-do men, believed to be on the Crown side, and included Michael Arnold, brewer of beer to the palace. He had been horrified. 'Whatever I do', he had said, 'I am sure to be half ruined. If I say "Not Guilty", I shall brew no more for the King; and if I say "Guilty", I shall brew no more for anybody else.'

11

. . . basins of water were sent in so that the jury might wash.

During most of that uncomfortable night, Mr Arnold said:
'Guilty.' At first nine were for acquitting and three for convict-
ing, but soon only Mr Arnold wanted to convict the bishops.
Thomas Austin, a large gentleman of great estate, had taken
notes at the trial and wanted to argue it out with him. But Mr
Arnold said he was not used to reasoning and debating, particularly when hungry. 'If you come to that', said Mr Austin,
as it grew light, 'look at me. I am the largest and strongest of
the twelve; and before I find such a petition as this to be a
libel, here I will stay till I am no bigger than a tobacco pipe.' At
six in the morning Mr Arnold yielded, and at ten in the
morning the foreman gave their verdict of 'Not Guilty', and
the bishops and the starving jury were freed.

Less than two hundred years later, hardship to the jury was
mitigated. By an Act of 1870 a jury was allowed a fire and
reasonable refreshments 'to be procured at their own
expense'; and soon after the practice grew up of a judge dis-
charging a jury altogether when disagreement seemed final,
and starting the case again with a new jury. Only in 1974 came
majority verdicts.

The courts used to sit enormously long hours by our stan-
dards, and a principal reason given for this was, ironically, the
convenience of jurors. From the moment a jury was sworn to
try the case until the verdict was given, the jurors in a trial for
felony – the more serious kind of crime – were not allowed to
separate. They were sometimes together for a long time, night
and day, being sent off at night to their unlit, unheated room.
It was not until an Act of 1897 that juries were allowed home at
night during trials for felony, and even then not in murder
cases.

In 1872, between the Acts of 1870 and 1897, Mr Arthur
Orton, a butcher from Wapping, who had claimed in intermin-
able civil proceedings to be Sir Roger Tichborne, a rich
baronet, was indicted for forgery and perjury. The forgery was
of certain bonds he had signed as Tichborne, the perjury consisted of claiming that he was Tichborne. The charges ran
together: the issues was the same: was he the long-lost Sir

Roger Tichborne or not ? Everybody knew the case would last a good six months. Forgery was a felony, perjury a mere misdemeanour. What was to be done with the jury? They could have fire and refreshments, if they could afford it, under the Act of 1870, but they could not separate and go home at night. The prosecution kindly dropped the charge of forgery, and Mr Orton was tried only for the misdemeanour. It was a wise decision. He was convicted on the 188th day of the hearing, and if he had been tried for forgery, the jury would have been locked up at night, week-ends and all, for 310 nights from 23 April 1873 until 28 February 1874.

The secrets of the jury room have rarely been betrayed but over the years they must include many intimate disasters. I am obliged to Lord Macaulay for one. 'Not even', he wrote woefully in his history, 'a candle to light a pipe was permitted to enter.'

2. Highwaymen and the Haymarket 1704 – 1769

Mr and Mrs Johnson brought an action against Mr Browning for malicious prosecution of Mrs Johnson. Chief Justice Holt laid down some rules of procedure worthy of the law report, and then reminisced of a case in the previous century. 'A son-in-law indicted his step-mother for poisoning her husband, his father; that she, being acquitted, brought an action for malicious prosecution against him, and recovered damages against him; that he, to requite her kindness, brought an appeal of murder; and that she was thereupon tried, and convicted at the King's Bench bar, and carried down, and burnt in Berkshire, where the fact was committed. And he remembered another very lately, where a fellow brought an action for saying of him, "he is a highwayman"; and it appearing upon evidence that he was so, he was taken in court; committed to Newgate; convicted at the next sessions; and hanged. So that people ought,' added the Chief Justice, 'to advise well before they bring such actions.'

Mr Darnell, counsel for Mr and Mrs Johnson, rather sanctimoniously I think, then joined in the morbid reminiscing with the remark that he 'remembered the like fate which befell a client of his'.

Lawyers can be at their most gruesome when happily remembering the past, and the most horrid disaster this book will record is noted by the great judge, Sir Matthew Hale, who condemned the two witches, in one almost throw-away sentence in his monumental *History of the Pleas of the Crown*. He sets out the law against gypsies, making them guilty of capital crime if they stayed in this country more than a month.

15

The law was passed in the reign of Queen Mary, and extended early in the reign of Queen Elizabeth to all 'that shall be found in the company of vagabonds, commonly called or calling themselves Egyptians, or counterfeiting or disguising themselves by their apparel, speech or behaviour like them, if they continue one month, although they are persons born in the King's dominions'. Sir Matthew, writing in the 1670s, a century later, comments: 'I have not known these statutes much put into execution, only about twenty years' since at the assizes at Bury about thirteen were condemned and executed for this offence'.

Another Act which remained in the statute book for an unconscionably long time was the one inspired by the Bishop of Rochester's cook in 1530. The cook, described in the Act as a man 'of the most wicked and damnable disposition', had put poison in the Bishop's porridge, so that those who ate on His Lordship's charity were envenomed and some died. The Act provided that the cook and future poisoners should be executed 'by boiling'. Into the pot went the cook, and at least two more poisoners, before Parliament in the reign of Edward VI passed another Act decreeing that poisoners should be hanged like other murderers. The first Act remained technically in force until it was repealed in 1863 but, thanks to the intervening Act, no later poisoners were lawfully boiled alive.

In 1725 two highwaymen fell out over the loot from their robberies. Joseph Williams sued John Everitt for £200; the action was not defended and Mr Williams obtained his judgment. Mr Everitt lived in fear of a debtor's prison, and was also exceedingly angry. He reckoned that Mr Williams had kept the greater part of their loot: much more than £200. So he consulted an attorney, William Wreathock, and that busy but ingenious man instructed Jonathan Collins of counsel to draw up a bill to start an action on the equity side, in the Court of Exchequer, for an account to be taken between the two rogues. Mr Collins must have had a lot of fun in chambers drafting the proceedings.

The statement of facts he drew sets out that 'your orator', John Everitt, is 'skilled in dealing and in buying and selling several sorts of commodities' and that Joseph Williams 'knowing your orator's great care diligence and industry in managing the said dealing' invited him into partnership. They agreed on this and further agreed that they should provide 'all sorts of necessaries at the joint and equal expense of both such as horses, bridles, saddles, assistants and servants'. The bill alleges 'that pursuant to the said agreement your orator and the said Joseph Williams went on and proceeded jointly in the said dealings with good success on Hounslow Heath where they dealt with a gentleman for a gold watch'. Later Mr Williams told Mr Everitt 'that Finchley was a good and convenient place to deal in' and so they 'dealt with several gentlemen for divers watches, rings, swords, canes, hats, cloaks, horses, bridles and other things to the value of £200 and upwards'. Then they met a gentleman at Blackheath 'and after some small discourse .... they dealt for his horse, bridle, saddle, watch, sword, cane and other things at a very cheap rate'. In pursuit of business they rode to Bagshot, Salisbury and Hampstead, and their profits were over £2,000. Mr Williams took charge of the goods, and Mr Everitt, finding that Mr Williams 'began to shuffle with him' asked for an account, but was refused. The bill ends with a fine formal flourish: Mr Everitt was without remedy at law and 'relievable only in a Court of Equity before Your Honours where just discoveries are made, frauds detected and just accounts stated'.

John Everitt's lawyers confidently expected that the threat of general exposure would bring about a settlement out of court. But Mr Williams kept his nerve and Mr Serjeant Girdler, on his behalf, persuaded the court to refer the bill to the Remembrancer for a report as being 'a scandal and an

17

They met a gentleman at Blackheath and . . . dealt for his horse . . . and
other things at a very cheap rate.

impertinence'. The action was dismissed. The Remembrancer reported and the court confirmed his report. A week later Mr Everitt's attorneys were brought before the court and fined £50 apiece, and Mr Jonathan Collins of counsel, who had kept discreetly away during the hearings, was ordered to pay the costs himself. I believe this to be the only case when a barrister was ordered to pay up. The final order ends with the words: 'and the court declares the indignity of the court as satisfied by the said fines and the deputy is not to consider the scandal in the taxation'.

Mr Williams was hanged for carrying out further business with travellers two years later, and he probably never got his £200. Mr Everitt's relief was short-lived, for in 1730 he was hanged for a highway robbery in Hampstead. In 1735 William Wreathock, the attorney, was himself condemned to death for a highway robbery, but reprieved, transported for life, returned with a royal pardon and practised again as a solicitor. It took a little while, but he was eventually struck off.

In the same year that the court so sanctimoniously condemned the time-wasting litigation between the two highwaymen, the highest lawyer in the land found himself on the wrong side of the law. Lord Macclesfield, the Lord Chancellor, fully realized what a peach of a job he had. Gracious and benign at the Opening of Parliament, he opened his speech with the words:

'My Lords and Gentlemen, I am persuaded you share in the satisfaction I feel at the prosperous situation of affairs: peace with all powers abroad; at home perfect tranquillity, plenty, and an uninterrupted enjoyment of all civil and religious rights – are most distinguishing marks of the favour and protection of Divine Providence.' Lord Macclesfield was asking for trouble; and he got it almost immediately.

Tom Parker was the son of a solicitor in Staffordshire. At twenty he set up as a solicitor himself. Five years later he was called to the bar. His ability brought him a heavy common law practice on the Midland Circuit. He became Serjeant Parker. He took a leading role in the impeachment of Dr Sacheverell (another disaster of the day): he was promptly made Chief Justice of the Queen's Bench. When George I landed at Greenwich, he was on the shore as a loyal Whig to greet him. The King spoke no English but took a liking to his Chief Justice, created him Lord Parker of Macclesfield, and arranged a pension of £1,200 a year to support the new dignity.

Lord Parker refused the offer of the Lord Chancellorship several times. A Chief Justice kept his post for life, whereas the Lord Chancellor fell with the Government. But in 1718 he finally agreed. It was a careful negotiation. The salary was £4,000 a year. In addition he got £2,000 for his new robes, £12,000 in cash from the King, the Earldom of Macclesfield and a pension for his son. It is impossible to compare the value of money then and now. But these were enormous sums and enough to catch a man whose ruling passion was money.

Lord Macclesfield was a sound judge. The Chancery Bar (we have heard this rather often) had doubts on the appointment of a common lawyer. They were not justified: his judgments were robust and clear. But among the officials whom he had power to appoint were the Masters in Chancery. These quiet men controlled the funds in court, whether paid in in the case of some endless litigation or on behalf of a child or a lunatic, or for a number of other purposes. The eighteenth century was not a time for bureaucratic controls or strict official integrity. The Masters had no duty to account for interest on the funds, or to provide proper accounts at all. They habitually took for themselves most of the income of the property they controlled, and when in 1720 the South Sea Bubble blew and joint stock companies flourished, the Masters joined enthusiastically in speculation. Inevitably there was much jostling for a post as Master, and no shortage of applicants prepared to pay for the privilege.

The Bubble burst. Master Fleetwood Dormer, in deficit by £25,000, fled to Holland. Lord Macclesfield had taken 3,000 guineas on two vacancies, and was anxious that there should be no scandal, making the posts unsaleable. 'Mr Dormer', he announced in court, 'has only gone to take the air in the country and will be back in a little time.' Mr Cottenham, Lord Macclesfield's confidential secretary, prepared for action.

When an applicant came forward for Mr Dormer's clearly vacant seat, the £5,000 tendered by him was graciously transferred towards the deficit on the basis that the other Masters paid the rest. Then Master Rogers decided to retire and agreed to sell his place for £6,000. The applicant went to see Cottenham, and offered a thousand guineas for the opportunity to buy. 'I couldn't mention it to My Lord under fifteen hundred,' said Cottenham. The actual price of purchase did not matter very much, as it could be recovered from the clients' funds, but the fifteen hundred had to be borrowed from the bank and passed to Cottenham, together with a bond for the future payment of the £6,000.

Master Hiccocks decided to sell, also for £6,000, to Master Benet's brother, Thomas, who offered £1,000 to Cottenham. 'That won't do, Mr Benet, you must be better advised,' said Cottenham. Benet asked Cottenham to ask the Lord Chancellor whether he would not take £1,000, but Cottenham stuck to his price. 'There is no haggling with My Lord; if you refuse it I don't know the consequence. He may resent it so as not to admit you at all.' 'Must I pay in gold?' 'In what you will, so it be guineas.' Benet borrowed the money from Master Hiccocks, who simply deducted it from the funds, before handing them over to his successor.

Then Master Fellowes died, and Mr Elde wanted the vacancy. He knew Lord Macclesfield and asked him directly to accept £5,000 for the job. 'You and I', said the Lord Chancellor, 'must not make bargains; but if you are desirous to have the office I will treat you in a different manner than I would any man living.' Elde called upon Cottenham in Westminster Hall, and asked his advice on how to go about it. 'Guineas are handsomer,' opined the secretary. So Mr Elde took a basket from his chambers, filled it with gold and notes, called at the house of the Lord Chancellor, found Cottenham in the hall, and delivered his basket. 'I saw him go upstairs with the basket', runs Mr Elde's later evidence, 'and when he came down he intimated that he had delivered it. When I was admitted, My Lord invited me to dinner and some of my friends with me, and he was pleased to treat me and some Members of the House of Commons in a very handsome manner. I was after dinner sworn in before them. Some months after I spoke to My Lord's gentleman, and desired him, if he saw such a basket, that he would give it me back. He did so, but no money was returned in it.'

Meanwhile the other Masters were having their problems. Lord Macclesfield was obliged to order one Master to pay out £1,000 to a suitor, from the suitor's own funds. The relevant Master had no money left. So Mr Cottenham went among them and suggested £50 a head contribution, with £500 from the one Master who had not contributed to the Dormer deficiency. They jibbed. Master Benet referred to a 'bottomless pit'.

Lord Macclesfield called a meeting of Masters. He sternly warned them against obduracy, but they were resolute. Lord Macclesfield paid up himself. But word was getting out, and the suitor for £1,000 promptly applied for a further payment. Counsel explained in court that there were rumours of a deficiency. Lord Macclesfield confessed that he too had heard such rumours – what knowledge he had was public news – he would refer the matter back to the Master for examination. The rumour enlarged like the Bubble itself. The First Minister, Robert Walpole, appointed a committee of the Privy Council, to be assisted by three judges and the Law Officers, to enquire and report to Parliament. Lord Macclesfield became distressed. He ordered the Masters to send in accounts of all trust monies, and to send the cash and securities in their control to the Bank of England, where it was to be kept in a chest with three locks, one to be kept by the Masters, one by

22

the six clerks of the Court of Chancery, one by the Governor of the Bank. But the tactic misfired. It was felt not to be the act of a disinterested public servant, but of a wrong-doer trying to cover up, and an admission of past embezzlement. The Ministers persuaded Lord Macclesfield to resign, hoping that this would end the public ill-will. It did not. The Committee reported on the deficit. It required payment of enormous sums to be authorized by Parliament.

In the House of Commons the storm burst with a Petition from the Earl of Oxford and Lord Morpeth, guardians of a lunatic, Elizabeth Dowager Duchess of Montague, stating that large sums paid to a Chancery Master had vanished. There was a debate, and furious speeches, which culminated in a decision by the House of Commons to impeach Lord Macclesfield before the House of Lords. A Bill was hastily passed into law, indemnifying the Masters and other witnesses against prosecution, whatever evidence they might give, and from then on Lord Macclesfield was doomed.

The trial took place in the House itself, the peers robed, the Commons as prosecutors. It lasted thirteen days and Master upon Master gave his evidence until everybody knew the price of each official post. Despite the weight of what they said, the impeachment might still have failed, impeachments always being pretty tricky, had not Lord Macclesfield performed at his most grandiose throughout. Mr Onslow, one of the managers for the Commons, remonstrated: 'The managers cannot but observe the indecent behaviour of this Lord, and his unworthy manner of treating us. We do not think the Lord at the bar should be directing the managers as if he sat in place as judge. We are here advocates for the Commons of Great Britain, to demand justice against him.'

On the whole though, the trial took place in a mood of good humour. The facts were too clear even for division on party lines. The defence indeed had its jolly aspect, based on evidence that other Lord Chancellors had from time to time sold posts, and on his Lordship's large contributions to charity. He made a very able and detailed speech in his own defence and declined to end with the usual peroration. 'My Lords, having thus gone through all my observations, it may be expected that I should close them by offering something in general : but I think it proper to forbear. I am not conscious myself that it is necessary in this case to apply to the passions, which is a common artifice to assist a weak defence.'

The peers convicted him dispassionately, fined him £30,000, and ordered him to be imprisoned in the Tower until the money had been paid. It took six weeks before he paid and was released, and for his seven remaining years of life he lived in seclusion in a small house near Derby, where his legal career had started. George I, still sympathetic, gave him £1,000 from his privy purse towards the fine and promised him more. But two years after the trial the King died and his successor was not minded to pay.

The suitors' funds were removed from the care of the Masters and placed in the Bank of England under the control of a new official, the Accountant General, an appointment obtained by one of the old Masters. The deficiency, of £100,871 6s 8d was paid from public money by the government, and then slowly recovered from future litigants by a tax on the sort of parchment used for writs. All the Masters kept their jobs, and all those admitted by Lord Macclesfield stayed on for twenty-five years at least. It was no disaster for the Masters, but it was for Lord Macclesfield, and a calamity for public respect for the law.

The dodge of keeping a rich defendant in the Tower until he has raised a huge fine might speed things up a little today.

When in 1738 Lord Mansfield was beginning to flourish at the bar, he acquired a new client, Sarah Duchess of Marlborough. She wished to litigate in chancery over the trusts in her

24

If they think they are going to find the barrister's clerk around at midnight . . .

husband's will. She sent him a general retainer of a thousand guineas. He returned 995 of them, five guineas being the cost of a general retainer. Lord Campbell tells the story:

'On one occasion, when late at night he came home to his chambers, he found them blocked by a splendid equipage; footman and pages, with torches in their hands, standing round; and the Duchess seated in his consulting chair. Instead of making any apology, she thus addressed him: "Young man, if you mean to rise in the world, you must not sup out." Another night, when, after the conclusion of a very long trial in which he had succeeded, he was indulging in agreeable conversation with Pope and Bolingbroke, Sarah again called, and having in vain expected his return till past midnight, went away without seeing him. His clerk, giving him an account of this visit next morning, said to him, "I could not make out, sir, who she was, for she would not tell me her name; but she swore so dreadfully that she must be a lady of quality."'

Nowadays the pop-star, the managers, the white Rolls-Royce may well want a conference in the Temple at very odd hours. If they think they are going to find the barrister's clerk around at midnight, they are in for further disaster.

'Single Joke' Lee was born in 1688, the year of the glorious Whig revolution and the accession of William III. Whenever he was asked his opinion on any public matter, he would merrily repeat that as he came in with King William he was bound to be a good Whig. Such simplicity combined with some pedantic learning was bound to take him far, and under the patronage of Lord Hardwicke he became a judge, and in 1737 Lord Chief Justice. All went well enough until the day in 1752 when he lost his nerve in court.

It was a political trial. The House of Commons had committed to prison a gentleman for failing to kneel when he appeared before them. William Owen, a bookseller, had published and sold copies of a pamphlet criticizing the Commons. The House directed the Attorney-General to prosecute Mr Owen, and he was sent for trial by jury before Lord Chief Justice Lee.

The Attorney-General argued that to convict him of criminal libel it was enough to prove that he had sold the book. The defence argued that the *book* had to be proved to be a libel. The Lord Chief Justice agreed with the prosecution and told the jury that they were bound to find him guilty as he admitted selling the book and he, the judge, had ruled as a matter of law that the book was libellous.

Two hours later the jury came back with their verdict.

CLERK OF THE COURT: Gentlemen of the jury, are you agreed on your verdict? Is the defendant guilty or not guilty?

FOREMAN: Guilty.

LORD CHIEF JUSTICE: You could not do otherwise.

JURYMEN (in chorus): No! No! My Lord! It is all a mistake – we say Not Guilty!

FOREMAN: Yes, My Lord, it was a mistake! I meant to say Not Guilty.

ATTORNEY-GENERAL (after cheers from the public gallery had subsided): My Lord, this must not be. I insist on the jury being called back and asked their opinion on the only question submitted to them.

LORD CHIEF JUSTICE (in obvious distress): Gentlemen of the jury, do you think the evidence laid before you of Owen's publishing the book by selling it is not sufficient to convince you that the said Owen did sell this book?

FOREMAN: Not Guilty, My Lord, Not Guilty!

JURYMEN (in chorus): That is our verdict, and so say we all.

There was applause in the court, and later bonfires in the street. It is recorded that from then on Lord Chief Justice Lee lost all authority and suffered constant mortification. Juries found verdicts contrary to his direction, and the bar paid him no deference.

Mr Baretti was a learned Italian aged fifty, long settled in London and the author of an Italian-English dictionary. One October afternoon in 1769 he was hurrying up the Haymarket on his way to meet some Royal Academicians when a woman on the pavement took hold of him, as a witness later declared, 'in a manner inconsistent with decency'. Mr Baretti was in sudden pain. She asked him for a glass of wine. Mr Baretti was distraught. She said he was 'a French *bougre*, a woman-hater' and should have 'a knock over the head with her patten'. He punched her. Instantly three men, Patman, Clark and Morgan, rushed upon him. They shoved him off the high pavement into the street. He pulled out his knife, struck Mr Patman and ran across the cobbles towards Panton Street. Mr Baretti was very short-sighted and frightened of a fall. He heard feet coming after him. Mr Baretti turned round and lunged with his knife. He stabbed Mr Morgan three times, and then fled into a grocer's shop, where shortly afterwards he gave himself up to a constable. Mr Morgan was carried off to the Middlesex Hospital, where he died of his wounds. Mr Baretti was committed for trial at the Old Bailey on a charge of murder.

It was then customary to offer a foreign defendant a jury composed half of Englishmen and half of foreigners, the feeling being that one foreigner was very much like another but trial should be by one's peers. But Mr Baretti rejected the offer, said he would prefer an honest English jury, and laid his plans. When an Italian acquaintance came to see him in his prison cell to ask for a letter of recommendation to his pupils to be used if Mr Baretti should be hanged, the answer was clear. 'You rascal, if I were not in my own apartment I would kick you down stairs directly.'

The prosecution evidence at trial, as we see it on paper, was formidable. An independent bystander gave evidence of Mr Baretti punching and stabbing away. Mr Patman and Mr Clark told their tale of innocence. Clark conceded that 'Morgan collared Baretti before he knew Patman was wounded'. All Morgan knew was that the foreigner had punched the woman. Mr Lambert, a tallow-chandler in Panton Street, also a constable, gave evidence of arrest. A patient from the hospital repeated the words of the dying Morgan: 'that he had gone to help two women whom the foreigner had assaulted, when he was suddenly stabbed three times, the last time worst of all'. Mr Wyatt, the surgeon who tended Morgan and dressed Patman's wound, gave more surprising evidence: Mr Wyatt had asked Clark if he knew the woman. Clark had denied it, but first admitted and then denied that Morgan had known her.

Mr Baretti was then allowed to read a statement from the dock. It was a clear account of what had happened: the insults from the woman, his pain and reaction, the chase, his panic, his regrets, the blows and whacks he had himself received. His lines have a somewhat Johnsonian ring: 'This, My Lord and gentlemen of the jury, is the best account I can give of my unfortunate accident: for what is done in two or three minutes, in fear and terror, is not to be minutely described; and the court and the jury are to judge. I hope Your Lordship, and every person present, will think that a man of my age, character, and way of life, would not spontaneously quit my pen to engage in an outrageous tumult. I hope it will easily be conceived that a man almost blind could not but be seized with terror at such a sudden attack as this. I hope it will be seen that my knife was neither a weapon of offence or defence; I wear it to carve fruit and sweetmeats, and not to kill my fellow creatures.'

Mr Baretti's distress was clear. His regret, he said, would endure as long as life should last, though the trial should turn out as favourably as innocence might deserve. His witnesses were called. Firstly came witnesses to shew, as they did, that he too had been bruised and struck about the face and body. Then came his friends, the learned world. 'Never', writes Boswell, 'did such a constellation of genius enlighten the awful Sessions House.' Boswell himself did not give evidence. Sir Joshua Reynolds, newly knighted and first President of the Royal Academy, discoursed of Mr Baretti's humanity, good temper, and sobriety. Dr Johnson was most careful of his answers, and perhaps more effective for that reason. It was the only occasion that he ever gave evidence. 'I have no reason to think he was ever disordered with liquor in his life. A man that I never knew to be otherwise than peaceable, and a man that I take to be rather timorous.'

COUNSEL (an interesting question for Boswell to consider):
    Was he addicted to pick up women in the street?
DR JOHNSON: I never knew that he was.
COUNSEL: How is he as to his eye-sight?
DR JOHNSON (himself half blind):   He does not see me now, nor do I see him. I do not believe he could be capable of assaulting anybody in the street without great provocation.

Edmund Burke, David Garrick, and Oliver Goldsmith followed Dr Johnson into the witness-box, and phrases such as remarkable humanity, good nature, active benevolence, a most peaceable man, resounded. Garrick even threw in a little social history. He testified that everyone abroad carried such a knife for in foreign inns only forks were provided.

COUNSEL: When you travel abroad do you carry such knives as this?
GARRICK: Yes, or we should have no victuals.

Mr Fitzherbert and Dr Hallifax, those learned clubmen, continued the procession. More were in the wings but the judge indicated that they had heard enough evidence of character. Whether the jury took a dim view of Morgan and his friends, whether they took a respectful view of this illustrious troupe of witnesses, we do not know; but they acquitted Mr Baretti, holding that he had acted in reasonable self-defence. But Mr

My Lord of London, chancing to remark
A noted Dean much busy'd in the Park . . .

Baretti meant it when he had said his regret would endure, and although his trial was a marked success he could never again bring himself to carry a knife, and was haunted by the run over the cobbles until he died, twenty years later.

Still with the eighteenth-century literati, here is Alexander Pope, giving Sober Advice from Horace to the Young Gentlemen about Town:

> My Lord of L—n, chancing to remark
> A noted Dean much busy'd in the Park,
> 'Proceed' (he cry'd) 'proceed, my Reverend Brother,
> 'Tis Fornicatio Simplex, and no other:
> Better than lust for Boys, with Pope and Turk,
> Or others' Spouses, like My Lord of York.'

It would be a winning entry in any competition to see how much actionable defamation you can get into six lines. The Dean, Thomas Sourbridge, Dean of Ferns and Leighlin, had actually been indicted for rape some four years before. No difficulty in identifying him. Edmund Gibson was Bishop of London. Archbishop Blackburne held the see of York, and, so rumour spoke, more than one mistress. No one, even the Pope, thought it wise to sue, and it was a disaster of missed opportunity for the lawyers.

3. A Long Story:
the Duchess-Countess
1776

On 15 April 1776 there opened in Westminster Hall a full dress rehearsal for the trial scene in *Alice*. The Queen and the Prince of Wales were there. A detachment of the guards had been sent by the King. Tickets changed hands at £20 apiece. Part of the public stand collapsed: a man's head was crushed. In an age of 'high towers of capillary ornament' the headdresses of many great ladies fragmented and fell. The peers assembled in their own House, and with the heralds and the ushers, they marched two by two to Westminster Hall.

The defendant was being bled by her doctor to lower her blood pressure, in a private room at Westminster. She was a comfortable-looking woman in her fifties, in widow's weeds; and she made her appearance in the Hall, attended by four ladies in waiting, three doctors and a clergyman. She was addressed by the high officials as Elizabeth Duchess of Kingston, and by the more cautious Lord High Steward as Madam. She was on trial for bigamy, and the issue for trial by her peers was whether she was a duchess or a countess.

Elizabeth Chudleigh was born about 1720, the daughter of a Lieutenant Governor of Chelsea Hospital, who lost his modest fortune in the South Sea Bubble, and promptly died. She was brought up by her mother in Devon in the simple manner of the age, so that when in her late adolescence she was out one day, and a middle-aged gentleman emerged with his gun and said to her: 'Madam, he is a fortunate hunter who can come out of a wood and meet a divinity', she knew just what was expected of her. The hunter was a rich and sophisticated politician, William Pulteney, later Earl of Bath, and when they eventually parted, he got her a post as maid of honour at the somewhat flashy court of the Princess of Wales, at a useful £400 per annum. The world of rich delinquents suited her. Some dukes were spurned by her but not many. The number of peers sitting in judgment upon her at Westminster Hall who had once been her lovers is uncertain. But at the start of her remarkable career she took an odd step.

In 1743 the nineteen-year-old Duke of Hamilton, 'hot, debauched and extravagant' in Walpole's words, proposed marriage to her. She accepted, and he was promptly sent off by his family on the Grand Tour. The following year she met Augustus Hervey, the second son of the Earl of Bristol, and a penniless naval lieutenant. She abandoned the Duke, whose passionate letters mysteriously failed to reach her, and married the sailor. It was a strange move for such a lady and she played it secretly. At eleven o'clock at night on 4 August 1744, she strolled casually out towards the summer-house at her aunt's house at Lainston in Hampshire, and was there married to Hervey by the Reverend Thomas Amis, the vicar of an adjoining parish. They stayed together for three days, and then Hervey returned to sea, and Elizabeth to her maidship of honour, which she would have lost had her marriage been known.

At Leicester House, at the party to celebrate the defeat of the Young Pretender, she led the ladies in firing sugar plums at an iced model of Carlisle Castle. She flirted with George II, who appointed her mother housekeeper at Windsor. On one occasion Hervey appeared from the sea. What happened between them is uncertain, but the marriage had wholly broken down when she gave birth to his child secretly in November 1747. To Elizabeth's relief the baby died and Hervey went back to sea, and did not pursue her again. The next great party was at Somerset House, where at the Venetian Ambassador's masque Elizabeth appeared in the role of Iphigenia, 'so naked', wrote Mrs Montague, 'that the high priest could very easily inspect the entrails of the victim'. The Princess of Wales threw a shawl over her in the ballroom, but this did not prevent Elizabeth acquiring a new lover, the Duke of Kingston.

When not in waiting, she lived with the Duke, and when he bought land at Prince's Gate, Knightsbridge, and built Kingston House upon it, she filled it with guests and trinkets. But as she approached forty, she began to hanker for respectability, by which she meant a lot of money and a genuine title. While she continued to be known as Miss Chudleigh she felt insecure and absurd. A possible solution emerged. In 1759, Hervey's elder brother George, then Earl of Bristol, was taken ill. Hervey was his heir. Elizabeth did not hesitate. She would rather, she decided, be the countess to an earl who now hated her, than the mistress to a duke who loved her. She drove to the Blue Boar, Winchester. She sent for Mrs Amis, wife of the now ailing clergyman who had married her. The marriage was so secret that it had never been registered. She visited Mr Amis. An attorney was fetched. She hid in a cupboard while transactions took place, and came back to London triumphant with a copy of her marriage lines in Mr Amis' hand. Then catastrophe – the Earl of Bristol recovered. Elizabeth had no option but to remain the smartest kept woman in London. She gave lavish parties, but the brilliance was now subdued. Lord Chesterfield, who had teased her about her secret child, now wrote: 'There is a thing called the decorum, and which I perceive the Duke of Kingston and Miss Chudleigh most scrupulously practise.' Fishing, a life-long passion, and visits to foreign courts took up much of her time.

Some years later another solution to her career problem was offered. Hervey now wanted to marry someone else, and he proposed to Elizabeth that he should obtain in the Ecclesiastical Court a decree of judicial separation based on her adultery, and thereafter a divorce by Act of Parliament. There was no divorce court in the eighteenth century; a special Act was the only way out. She could prove her own adultery. Elizabeth, rather oddly, was indignant: she refused to 'prove herself a whore'. She made a counter-proposal on the advice of her lawyers. She would bring in the Ecclesiastical Court an action for jactitation of marriage, that is an action for a declaration that he was wrongly boasting or claiming to be her husband. He would not defend her claim. He was to bring a cross-action, claiming the rights of marriage, but was not to support it with evidence. She would win, and the marriage, said the lawyers, would be as if it had never taken place. Elizabeth would forget the visit to Winchester. In 1769 in the action and cross-action the Ecclesiastical Court declared that Elizabeth Chudleigh 'was, and now is, a spinster, and free from all matrimonial contracts'. As neither party had even attempted to prove the marriage, and there was no evidence before the court of the corrupt bargain which had been struck between the parties, it is difficult to see what else the Ecclesiastical Court could have done.

Justice had miscarried but the law had gone through its forms and on 8 March 1769 a ceremony of marriage was performed between Elizabeth and the Duke of Kingston. In July 1770 the Duke made a will in her favour. He left her his personal estate without reservation, pictures, jewellery, furniture, money, the lot. He left her during her widowhood his real estate with its rents and profits. He cut out his elder nephew, Evelyn. His younger nephew, Charles, was to get the real estate on Elizabeth's death or the determination of her widowhood. He left this splendid fortune to her as 'Elizabeth Duchess of Kingston, my wife'. But supposing she was not his legal wife, and on his death was not his widow? There had been no Act of Parliament, no divorce from Hervey. It all turned on whether the declaration of the Ecclesiastical Court that Elizabeth had never been married to Hervey could be proved to have been obtained by a secret and corrupt bargain between them, and even if so, whether the declaration still bound the civil and criminal courts so that they could not enquire into the true facts. Evelyn had, in his injured pride, as strong a motive as Charles, the residual heir, in challenging the will.

In 1773 the Duke was struck with a palsy and died, and Evelyn set to work. He had four aims: (a) to prove the Hervey marriage of 1744, (b) to expose the collusive and dis-

36

honest nature of the Ecclesiastical Court proceedings, (c) to get Elizabeth convicted of bigamy, and (d) to set aside the Duke's will.

While Evelyn plotted, Elizabeth travelled. She was immensely rich and treated as royalty wherever she went. 'She is gone back to the Continent', wrote one of the peers, 'and her return (if ever) uncertain. Russia is mentioned as a country she is likely to go to. When she waited on the Pope at Rome, where she was going to buy a villa and dig for antiquities, she told His Holiness that there was no coming to Jerusalem without adoration. The Villa Negroni is, I believe, what she was in treaty for.'

On 18 March 1775 the Earl of Bristol died at last, and was succeeded by Hervey. So if she had never been a duchess, Elizabeth now become a genuine countess. But it was too late for respectability. A grand jury committed her for trial for bigamy. In Rome she was told that she must return to face the charge or she would be outlawed. She determined to return. She hurried to Mr Jenkins, her banker in Rome, to collect her money and jewels. He hesitated. She burst in upon him with a pair of loaded pistols. He hesitated no longer, and Elizabeth with all her assets came back to England. She still had many supporters. Three duchesses called upon her. A duke stood bail. Lord Mansfield, the Lord Chief Justice, not only granted bail but invited her to sit on the bench with him. She tried to persuade the Attorney-General to stop the case on the basis of the findings of the Ecclesiastical Court, but it had all gone too far and excited preparations began for the most lavish of English trials, trial by her peers.

The punishment for bigamy in the eighteenth century was still branding on the hand. But as a peeress, and on first conviction, she could claim benefit of peerage and go unscathed and unsentenced. If not a duchess she was still a countess. The trial was a folly. Lord Mansfield spelled it out in the House of Lords: 'The arguments about the place of trial suggest to my mind a question about the propriety of any trial at all. *Cui bono?* What utility is to be obtained? Supposing a conviction be the result? The lady makes your lordships a curtsy, and you return a bow.' But peers and public were not to be deprived of a party way beyond the splendid entertainments of Leicester and Somerset Houses, and some four thousand spectators crammed into Westminster Hall to see the fun.

The celebrated adventuress conducted herself with strict propriety, bowing, curtsying, kneeling as indicated to her. After the reading of lengthy charges and writs she was asked if she was guilty. She said she was not.

Ann Craddock, servant to Elizabeth's aunt, said she had been present at the Hervey marriage, had seen the pair in bed together, and that Elizabeth had told her of her child by Hervey. She was questioned by a dozen peers but unshaken in her evidence. Elizabeth's doctor gave evidence of the child and of Elizabeth's admission of the marriage. The gentry were more reluctant to prove the facts, and this alone set the peeresses against Elizabeth. 'The invidious spleen of the peeresses, not the justice of the peers, are her untameable persecutors,' wrote one male worthy. Lord Barrington, an old admirer of Elizabeth, fell into deep waters.

LORD BARRINGTON: My Lords, I think every man must act from his own feelings, and I feel that any private conversation entrusted to me is not to be reported again.
A LORD: His Lordship will recollect the oath that he has taken, that he shall declare the whole truth.

Elizabeth rapidly intervened. It is one of the passages in the trial where she appears as a born advocate. 'I do release My Lord Barrington from every obligation of honour,' she declared. 'I wish, and earnestly desire, that every witness who shall be examined may deliver their opinions in every point justly, whether for me or against me. I came from Rome at the hazard of my life to surrender myself to this court. I bow with submissive deference to every decree, and do not even complain that an ecclesiastical sentence has been deemed of no force, although such a sentence has never been contraverted during the space of one thousand four hundred and seventy-five years.'

Like other born advocates, Elizabeth overdid it. She had lost the sympathy of the court. Meanwhile Their Lordships carried on a spirited discussion as to whether the noble witness should be expected to breach gentlemanly confidences.

The Solicitor-General, who had called Lord Barrington, eventually decided he was going to do the Crown case no good. He proposed to ask him no more questions, but to let Elizabeth's counsel, Mr Wallace, cross-examine him if he chose. Mr Wallace said he did not choose to do so. But the peers were in no mood to let it go.

DUKE OF RICHMOND: I would ask the noble Lord whether he knows any fact by which he is convinced that Mr Hervey was married to Miss Chudleigh.

LORD BARRINGTON (cautiously):   I do not know of any fact which will prove the marriage between the Duchess of Kingston and Mr Hervey of my own knowledge.

DUKE OF RICHMOND: The noble Lord must leave it to the house to judge whether it will or not. But does His Lordship know any fact relative to the matter?

LORD BARRINGTON: I do not know anything of my own knowledge that can tend to prove the marriage. I know nothing but what I have heard in the world and from conversation.

LORD RADNOR: I am afraid Your Lordships, by your acquiescence, have admitted a rule of proceeding here which would not be admitted at any inferior court in the kingdom. I desire, therefore, to ask the noble Lord whether he knows any matter of fact relative to that marriage.

LORD BARRINGTON: My Lords, if I do, I cannot reveal it, nor can I answer the question without betraying private conversation.

The House then adjourned to consider how far a gentleman should be expected to betray confidences in a court, and reached the conclusion, inevitable in English law, that the witness had no such privilege and must answer all questions.

Both counsel promptly repeated that they had no questions to ask, and Lord Radnor returned to the attack. Lord Barrington's memory then failed him, or possibly clarified. . . .

LORD BARRINGTON: The Duchess of Kingston has never communicated to me, in the course of her life, to the best of my knowledge and belief, anything which was, at the time she was pleased to communicate it to me, in the least a deviation from the strictest rules of virtue and religion.

On the fifth and final day of the trial Elizabeth addressed her peers herself, with dignity, some ingenuity and at considerable length. She did not in terms dispute the Hervey marriage, the child, the secret visit to Winchester. She then raised her best defence. To prove bigamy, she said, the prosecution must establish a criminal and wicked intent. She had acted always on legal advice, and she and that honourable man, the late Duke of Kingston, who had known all the facts, had believed that they were free to marry. If they were mistaken, there was no criminal intent. 'Where such intention does not exist, your Lordships' justice and humanity will tell you there can be no crime; and Your Lordships, looking on my distressed situation with an indulgent eye, will pity me as an unfortunate woman, deceived and misled by erroneous notions of law, of the propriety of which it was impossible for me to judge.'

But no indulgent eye shone. The unhelpful attitude of Lord Barrington, Elizabeth's obvious shrewdness, rumours of attempts by Elizabeth to suborn the witnesses, did not endear her to them. Their Lordships rightly concluded that the ecclesiastical proceedings were fraudulent, in that Elizabeth and Hervey had corruptly agreed to deceive the Ecclesiastical Court, so as to enable Elizabeth to marry her Duke.

After Elizabeth's address came her witnesses. They added nothing. The Lord High Steward promptly called upon each peer, starting with the youngest, to stand up, uncover his head, lay his right hand upon his breast, and declare his verdict. Each peer obeyed the instruction, answering: 'Guilty, upon my honour', save for the loyal Duke of Newcastle, who

She bought an estate in Russia, which she named Chudleigh. She established a vodka factory.

had stood bail for Elizabeth, was the county neighbour of the Duke of Kingston, and a former lover of his Duchess. 'Guilty erroneously', he said, 'but not intentionally.'

Elizabeth was brought to the bar and asked if she had anything to say. She produced a paper by which she claimed benefit of peerage. The Attorney-General was asked if he had anything to say. He sounded rather bewildered again. 'My Lords, not expecting to be called upon, I did not attend to the form of words used by the prisoner.' However, he then spoke for about an hour, and worked up to a passionate demand for the burning of Elizabeth's hand.

Whether Duchess or Countess, Elizabeth was allowed to enjoy the benefit of peerage, and no punishment could be forced on her. The reports do not indicate whether the lady made their Lordships a curtsy, and, if so, whether they returned a bow, but the party was over at last, and, as Lord Mansfield suggested, to no useful purpose. Elizabeth felt herself wholly undefeated, save on a legal technicality. The nephews issued a writ to prevent her leaving the country, but while her splendid carriage was driven slowly Knightsbridge-wards, with a solitary veiled occupant, Elizabeth was driven at top speed to Dover, sailed for Calais, and never returned. She kept the cash. At Munich the Elector created her Countess of Warth. At Vienna the Papal Nuncio asked the Pope to intervene to persuade the Empress Maria Theresa to receive her as a duchess. Near Riga, Prince Radziwill held an elaborate boar-hunt and created a toy village in her honour. At St Petersburg the Empress Catherine provided her with a mansion. She bought an estate in Russia, which she named Chudleigh. She established a vodka factory. She then transferred herself to France, acquired huge properties and eccentric lovers, and in 1786 'by the last will and testament of the most noble Elizabeth Duchess of Kingston in England, Countess of Warth in the Electorate of Bavaria, and Duchess of Kingston in Russia', she made typically generous provisions for the nephews and their children. It was a case of disaster being blandly ignored.

4. The Scots Are Ruder
1777 – 1800

The Reverend Doctor William Dodd was a clergyman of mixed reputation. Editor of the *Christian Magazine*, Prebendary of Brecon, Chaplain to the King, he was struck off the list of royal chaplains when he offered 3,000 guineas to the wife of the Lord Chancellor to procure him the living of St George's, Hanover Square. He founded the Charlotte Chapel in the Italianate suburb of Pimlico, and for this was known as the 'macaroni clergyman'. He was a fashionably shocking preacher, but found himself described in Goldsmith's *Retaliation* as a 'quacking divine'. He was taken on as tutor to the young Earl of Chesterfield and seen and heard everywhere.

In 1777 he found he owed his tradesmen some £300. To cover this modest sum, he took a devious course. He told Mr Robertson, a bill-broker, that the young Earl urgently needed £4,000. He did not tell the young Earl. Mr Robertson found some lenders and asked Dr Dodd to get a bond executed. Dr Dodd returned it signed Chesterfield and witnessed by himself. Mr Robertson, thinking two witnesses better than one, added his own name as a witness. Dr Dodd received £4,200, of which he gave Mr Robertson £100 as commission.

A lawyer to one of the lenders thought the bond looked a bit messy and advised the lender to take it back to the Earl and get a clean one. The Earl disowned it. The lenders and their lawyers rushed to Guildhall and laid charges of forgery against Mr Robertson and Dr Dodd. Mr Robertson was taken into custody; and then they all moved on to Dr Dodd's house. Dr Dodd was very agreeable and apologetic. When they told him that he would be saved from the gallows if he repaid the money in full, he hastily borrowed and arranged the repayment in full. Then he was taken before the Lord Mayor, where he again explained and apologized, but was committed for trial for forgery.

The trial began with a technical wrangle. Was the case against Dr Dodd a nullity because the name of Mr Robertson, the broker, was put on the back of the indictment as a prosecution witness, and was not Mr Robertson ineligible to give evidence, being a defendant himself? It was the sort of point pleasing to the eighteenth century, and it was argued for hours. The conclusion was that the knotty point would be reserved for the opinion of twelve judges, and meanwhile Dr Dodd would be tried.

There was really no defence to a charge of forgery. The fact that the money had been repaid, the fact that Dr Dodd had always meant to repay it, was relevant to sentence but not to the question the jury had to answer, whether he was guilty of forgery. The witnesses gave their evidence. Dr Dodd made a short and rather muddled speech. The jury found him guilty but recommended him to royal mercy.

Some three months later he was brought back from prison to the Old Bailey and told that the judges had decided against him on the technical point which had been reserved, and soon afterwards he was brought up to receive his sentence.

This time his speech was eloquent. It was in fact written by Dr Johnson, who had no great affection for Dr Dodd or his style of life, but felt much agitated at his being hanged. 'I was not an idle, nor, I hope, an useless minister: I taught the truths of Christianity with the zeal of conviction, and the authority of innocence. My labours were approved; my pulpit became popular; and, I have reason to believe, that of those who heard me some have been preserved from sin, and some have been reclaimed. Condescend, My Lord, to think, if these considerations aggravate my crime, how much they must embitter my punishment.'

Dr Dodd was sentenced to death, and a vast agitation arose to obtain the King's mercy for him, as the jury had recom-

. . . the privilege of riding in his own carriage with a hearse containing his coffin preceding him.

mended. Dr Johnson wrote a sermon for him to deliver in Newgate and drafted letters to the King and Queen on his behalf. A petition for mercy was signed by twenty thousand people, and it is arguable that Dr Dodd's execution was the birth of public opposition to capital punishment.

For executed he was. There was an enormous crowd, and instead of travelling in the usual tumbril from Newgate to Tyburn, manacled and seated on his coffin, Dr Dodd was allowed the privilege of riding in his own carriage with a hearse containing his coffin preceding him. Whether the King, and Lord Mansfield who advised him, were determined to be consistent in capital punishment for all classes of society, or were simply shocked by forgery, cannot now be ascertained ; but Dr Dodd had done no real harm, and no one had lost any money.

Go any day into a law court where an action is being tried, civil, criminal or divorce, and you will hear a witness repeating what was said on some occasion a year or more ago. It may have been something of no significance then to the witness, or something of considerable length, but our legal system is based on the curious notion that people can remember whole sentences for a remarkably long time. Outside the law courts and occasionally within, we realize that we do not normally recollect the precise words of a conversation ten minutes after they were spoken, even if we remember the gist. Hence the vital importance of a note made at the time. But note-taking can work against the credibility of a witness.

In 1780 the fanatical Lord George Gordon led a violent protest against the repeal of certain anti-Catholic laws. The 'No Popery' riots which followed caused the most visible devastation to London between the Great Fire of 1666 and the blitz of 1940. Lord George stood trial for high treason, charged

with levying war against the King, and his defence, strenu-
ously argued by counsel, was that his intentions had been
wholly peaceful, and the mob had been carried away of its own
accord. So all turned on what Lord George had actually said.

The star witness for the Crown was William Hay, a printer.
He remembered precisely what Gordon had said at mass
meetings: 'The King has broken his coronation oath'; 'By ass-
enting to the Act for tolerating Catholics, the King has brought
himself to the same pass as James II after his abdication', 'Stick
steadily to your good and glorious cause'.

KENNYON, counsel for the defendant: When did you first
resort to these Protestant meetings?

HAY: On the tenth of the December before the riots.

KENNYON: And then you attended others, at some of which
Lord George was present, at some of which he was not?

HAY: Yes, he was not present at all the meetings.

KENNYON: Just now you told my learned friend that Lord
George was present at a meeting on 21 January?

HAY: Yes.

KENNYON: Reflect carefully. Did you see him there or not?

HAY: I think I saw him there.

KENNYON: Be on your guard. Did you see him there or not?

HAY (the moment of disaster): I could speak with more certainty if I might look at my notes.

KENNYON: Notes? Notes? How came you to take notes?

HAY: I will tell you very freely. Originally, my curiosity led
me to those meetings, but in time I came to dread and
foresee the consequences of them.

KENNYON: When did you first foresee the consequences?

HAY: At a meeting on the twentieth of February.

KENNYON: If that was the first time you were moved to take
notes, how would your notes help you with the twenty-first
of January?

HAY: I took notes at all the meetings right from the tenth of
December.

KENNYON: Why did you take notes before you foresaw the

consequences?

HAY: Whenever I go to public meetings, I take notes.

KENNYON: Give me an instance, other than these. Tell me where and when you have taken notes before.

No answer.

KENNYON: Tell me where and when.

No answer.

KENNYON: Tell me where and when.

HAY (improbably): At the General Assembly of the Church of Scotland. When I was much younger – twenty-two years ago.

Lord George Gordon was acquitted. Whether because the jury were religious bigots, or did not care for the evidence of a spy I do not know. But for Mr Hay, his note-taking was more of a disaster than if he had not taken notes.

If you have sat on a jury you will have heard the judge tell you that the law is for him and the facts are for you, that he will direct you on the law and you must accept his rulings, and then it is for you to decide the facts and apply the law as he has declared it. 'If I am wrong on the law', he may add with a flourish heavenward, 'there is another court to put it right.'

But suppose, when the jury retires, you all conclude that the judge has got the law wrong, or that his rulings on law offend your common sense of justice; and you acquit in disregard of his rulings? Your verdict remains final, and you win. In the celebrated trial in 1788 of the Dean of St Asaph for seditious libel, our greatest advocate, Henry Erskine, actually invited the jury to disregard the judge's rulings of law. The Dean was convicted and on an application by Erskine for a new trial, counsel for the Crown, Mr Bearsted, conceded that the jury had the right to take upon themselves the decision of every question of law necessary to the acquittal of the defendant, and the famous Lord Mansfield observed that 'he should call it the power, not the right'. A young barrister, John Clerk, decided to try the Erskine line before Lord Braxfield and the Scottish judges.

At the time of the joint trial of Deacon Brodie and George Smith, John Clerk had been at the bar for less than three years. It was a notorious case. Deacon Brodie, on whom Stevenson was to model Dr Jekyll and Mr Hyde, was a merchant, councillor and clubman of Edinburgh. He was charged together with Smith with breaking into the General Excise Office for Scotland. He was suspected of a whole series of burglaries and robberies, committed with Smith and with two other disreputable characters, Ainslie and Brown, who were allowed to save themselves by giving vital evidence for the prosecution. On behalf of the Deacon, the services of the Dean of Faculty, the leader of the bar, Erskine himself, were retained. Smith, less substantial, was represented by young John Clerk, lame, plain and enthusiastic. Early in the trial Erskine and Clerk objected to the admission of the evidence of Ainslie and Brown, as they were clearly accomplices in the crime. Lord Braxfield and the four other judges ruled against them. At about two in the morning, fortified by a bottle of claret, Clerk rose to address the jury on behalf of Smith. He began by referring to his own inexperience.

LORD BRAXFIELD: Be short and concise, sir, at this hour of the morning.
CLERK: Pray, Your Lordship, let me proceed.
LORD BRAXFIELD: Well then, proceed, young man.

Clerk steadily proceeded, and among the flickering candles, firmly asserted that Their Lordships should not have allowed Ainslie and Brown to give evidence.

Lord Braxfield: Do you say that, sir, after the judgment which the court has pronounced? That, sir, is a most improper observation to address at the outset to the jury.

Lord Stonefield: It is a positive reflection on the court.

Lord Hailes: It is a flat accusation that we have admitted improper evidence.

Lord Eskgrove: I never heard the like of this from any young counsel at the beginning of his career at this bar.

Lord Braxfield: With these admonitions, go on, sir; proceed, sir.

Clerk: Aweel, My Lords, if I go on, I beg to assail at the outset the evidence of these two corbies or infernal scoundrels, Ainslie and Brown.

Lord Braxfield: Take care, sir, what you say.

Clerk: Yes, My Lords, I say that they are both most infamous characters. Gentlemen, you should discard such vagabonds, and not rely on their evidence in any way; and if you knock out the vile brains of their evidence in this case, there is nothing else remaining on which you can convict my poor client, except his own very candid declarations which I have already explained to you. Gentlemen, these nefarious witnesses Ainslie and Brown should have stood at this bar this night in place of my client, who was happy in his domestic privacy with his poor, honest, inoffending wife, whom you this day saw – and my heart bleeds for her. (Public applause suppressed.) Gentlemen, Ainslie contradicts himself, and Brown is not to be believed. With respect to this said Mr John Brown alias Humphrey Moore, you had it out of his own mouth that he was a convicted felon in England, and I say to you that no convicted felon ought, by the good and glorious law of Scotland, to be received as a witness in this or in any other case in the British dominions. (Great applause suppressed.)

Lord Braxfield: Mr Clerk, please restrict your reflections. The court has admitted the witness.

Clerk: Yes, My Lords. I know that very well, but Your Lordships should *not* have admitted him, and of that the

50

jury will now judge.

LORD BRAXFIELD: This is most indecent behaviour. You cannot be allowed to speak to the admissibility; to the credibility you may.

LORD STONEFIELD: This young man is again attacking the court.

CLERK: No, My Lords, I am not attacking the court; I am attacking that villain of a witness, who, I tell Your Lordships, is not worth his value in hemp.

LORD BRAXFIELD: The court, sir, have already solemnly decided, as you know, on the objections raised by the Dean of Faculty, that in law the objections to these witnesses should be repelled, and they were repelled accordingly; therefore you should have nothing more to say to us on that point.

ERSKINE, DEAN OF FACULTY: If it will satisfy Mr Clerk, I can assure him that I will plead on this point to the jury, waiving all objections to the admissibility, which it may be rather irregular to plead after the decision of the court.

LORD BRAXFIELD: Dean of Faculty, I know *you* will attempt nothing that is improper.

CLERK: But, My Lords, the jury are to judge of the law as well as the facts.

LORD BRAXFIELD: Sir I tell you that the jury have nothing to do with the law, but to take it *simpliciter* from me.

CLERK: That I deny.

If the ceiling cracked asunder at this point, the court seems physically to have remained intact.

LORD HAILES (slowly): Sir, will you deny the authority of this High Court?

CLERK: Gentlemen of the jury, notwithstanding of this interruption, I beg to tell you, with all confidence and all respect, that you are the judges of the law as well as the facts. You are the judges of the whole case.

LORD BRAXFIELD: You are talking nonsense, sir.

CLERK: My Lord, you had better not snub me in this way. I never mean to speak nonsense.

51

Junior counsel : But, My Lords, the jury are to judge of the law as well as the facts.

Lord Braxfield : Sir I tell you that the jury have nothing to do with the law, but to take it *simpliciter* from me.

LORD BRAXFIELD: Proceed – gang on, sir.

CLERK: Gentlemen, I was telling you that this infernal witness was convicted of felony in England, and how dare he come here to be received as a witness in this case?

LORD ADVOCATE (for the Crown): He has, as I have shown you, received His Majesty's free pardon.

CLERK: Yes, I see; but gentlemen of the jury, I ask you, on your oaths, can His Majesty make a tainted scoundrel an honest man?

The ceiling still did not fall in. There was great applause.

LORD BRAXFIELD: Macers, clear the court if there is any more unruly din.

LORD ADVOCATE: Sir, permit me to say, after this interruption, that the prerogative of mercy is the brightest jewel in His Majesty's Crown.

CLERK: I hope His Majesty's Crown will never be contaminated by any villains around it.

LORD BRAXFIELD (to the Lord Advocate, the Scottish Attorney-General): Do you want his words noted down?

LORD ADVOCATE: Oh no, My Lord, not exactly yet. My young friend will soon cool in his effervescence for his client.

LORD BRAXFIELD (back to Clerk): Go on, young man.

CLERK: Gentlemen of the jury, I was just saying to you, when this outbreak on the bench occurred, that you were the judges of the law and of the facts in this case.

LORD BRAXFIELD: We cannot tolerate this, sir. It is an indignity to this High Court – a very gross indignity, deserving of the severest reprobation.

CLERK: My Lords, I know that Your Lordships have determined this question; but the jury have not. They are judges both of fact and of the law, and are not bound by Your Lordships' determination, unless it agrees with their own opinion. Unless I am allowed to speak to the jury in this manner, I am determined not to speak a word more. I am willing to sit down if Your Lordships command me.

Mr Clerk sat down.

LORD BRAXFIELD: Go on, sir; go on to the length of your tether.

Mr Clerk stood up.

CLERK: Yes, gentlemen, I stand up here as an independent Scottish advocate, and I tell you, a jury of my countrymen, that you are the judges of the law as well as of the facts.
LORD BRAXFIELD: Beware of what you are about, sir.

Mr Clerk sat down.

LORD BRAXFIELD: Are you done, sir, with your speech?
CLERK: No, My Lord, I am not.
LORD BRAXFIELD: Then go on, sir, at your peril.
LORD HAILES: You had better go on, Mr Clerk. Do go on.
CLERK: This has been too often repeated. I have met with no politeness from the court. You have interrupted me, you have snubbed me rather too often, My Lord, in the line of my defence. I maintain that the jury are judges of the law as well as of the facts; and I am positively resolved that I will proceed no further unless I am allowed to speak in my own way.
LORD BRAXFIELD: Then we must now call upon the Dean of Faculty to proceed with his address for the prisoner Brodie, which the court will hear with the greatest attention.

Erskine shook his head from side to side. Lord Braxfield drew himself up to begin his summing-up.

CLERK (jumping up and shaking his fist): Hang my client if you daur, My Lord, without hearing me in his defence.

The judges had never heard anything like it. They rose and retired to their private room. When they returned, Lord Braxfield merely invited Mr Clerk to proceed with his speech; and quite quietly Clerk proceeded.

But it got him nowhere. His client and the Deacon were convicted and hanged. Lord Braxfield has passed down to history and legend as the most coarsely ferocious of Scottish judges. John Clerk became Solicitor-General for Scotland, and later, as a judge himself, Lord Eldin.

My favourite forensic row is not likely to be replaced. The courts now rise for the day at tea-time, and counsel never harangue the judges at two in the morning.

But more of Lord Braxfield, whose Scottish accent is faithfully copied in the reports. Born Robert McQueen, Lord Braxfield was the model for Stevenson's Weir of Hermiston, and for all later judges who thought themselves robust and were found overbearing. 'He was like a formidable blacksmith,' wrote Lord Cockburn, 'his accent and his dialect were exaggerated Scotch; his language, like his thoughts, short, strong, and conclusive.' When two counsel appeared in his court suffering from a rough night: 'Gentlemen, ye may just pack up your papers and gang home; the tame o' ye's riftin' punch and the itter's belchin' claret – there'll be nae guid got oot o' ye the day.' In one of the sedition trials of the 1790s, a defendant maintained to the jury that all great men had been reformers, 'even Our Saviour himself'. 'Muckle he made a' that,' muttered Lord Braxfield, 'He was haangit.'

But under attack he was less formidable, and the trial for sedition of Mr Margarot had its moment of disaster both for the defendant and for Lord Braxfield, Lord Justice-Clerk. It was a moment unique in the history of cross-examination, when the defendant turned on the judge.

MARGAROT: Now, My Lords, comes a very delicate matter indeed. I mean to call upon my Lord Justice-Clerk, and I hope that the questions and the answers will be given in a most solemn manner. I have received a piece of information which I shall lay before the court in the course of my questions. First, My Lord, are you upon oath?

LORD BRAXFIELD: State your questions, and I will tell you

whether I will answer them or not. If they are proper questions I will answer them.

MARGAROT: Did you dine at Mr Rocheid's at Inverleith in the course of last week?

LORD BRAXFIELD: And what have you to do with that, sir?

MARGAROT: Did any conversation take place with regard to my trial?

LORD BRAXFIELD: Go on, sir.

MARGAROT: Did you use these words: What would you think of giving him a hundred lashes, together with Botany Bay; or words to that effect?

LORD BRAXFIELD: Go on. Put your questions if you have any more.

MARGAROT: Did any person – did a lady – say to you that the mob would not allow you to whip him? And, My Lord, did you not say that the mob would be the better for losing a little blood? These are the questions, My Lord, that I wish to put to you at present in the presence of the Court. Deny them, or acknowledge them.

LORD BRAXFIELD (somewhat shaken): Do you think I should answer questions of that sort, My Lord Henderland?

Lord Henderland, his colleague, thought, on the whole, not. Mr Margarot was transported for fourteen years, and survived to return home, turn Tory, and give evidence about transportation before a Committee of the House of Commons.

Back in England legal disasters were going through a more light-hearted phase, and I am indebted to Lord Campbell's *Lives of the Chief Justices* which he wrote during the 1850s. He describes the habit of two succeeding Lord Chief Justices, Lord Kenyon, who held office from 1788 to 1802, and Lord

Ellenborough, who resigned in 1818.

'In those days retiring-rooms for the use of the judges were unknown, and a porcelain vase, with a handle to it, was placed in a corner of the court at the extremity of the bench. In the King's Bench at Guildhall the students' box (in which I myself have often sat) was very near this corner. One day a student who was taking notes, finding the ink in his little ink-bottle very thick, used the freedom secretly to discharge the whole of it into My Lord's porcelain vase. His Lordship soon after having occasion to come to this corner, he was observed in the course of a few moments to become much disconcerted and distressed. In truth, discovering the liquid with which he was filling the vase to be of a jet-black colour, he thought the secretion indicated the sudden attack of some mortal disorder. In great confusion and anguish of mind he returned to his seat and attempted to resume the trial of the cause but, finding his hand to shake so much that he could not write, he said that on account of indisposition he was obliged to adjourn the court. As he was led to his carriage by his servants, the luckless student came up and said to him, 'My Lord, I hope Your Lordship will excuse me, as I suspect that I am unfortunately the cause of Your Lordship's apprehensions.' He then described what he had done, expressing deep contrition for his thoughtlessness and impertinence, and saying that he considered it his duty to relieve His Lordship's mind by his confession. Lord Kenyon: 'Sir, you are a man of sense and a gentleman – dine with us on Sunday.' Lord Ellenborough pursued the same practice. I myself have often heard his large seals dangling from his watch-chain rattle against the vase, as he took it in his hand *coram populo*, decorously turning his back upon them.'

Lord Ellenborough features again in *Table Talk*, a book of reminiscences by Samuel Rogers, the Regency poet:

'Lord Ellenborough was once about to go on the circuit, when Lady Ellenborough said that she should like to accompany him. He replied that he had no objection, provided she did not encumber the carriage with bandboxes, which were his

. . . decorously turning his back upon them.

utter abhorrence. During the first day's journey, Lord Ellenborough, happening to stretch his legs, struck his foot against something below the seat. He discovered that it was a bandbox. Up went the window and out went the bandbox. The coachmen stopped, and the footmen, thinking that the bandbox had tumbled out of the window by some extraordinary chance, were going to pick it up, when Lord Ellenborough furiously called out, 'Drive on!' The bandbox accordingly was left by the ditch-side. Having reached the county town where he was to officiate as judge, Lord Ellenborough proceeded to array himself for his appearance in the courthouse. 'Now,' said he, 'where's my wig – where *is* my wig?' 'My Lord,' replied his attendant, 'it was thrown out of the carriage window.'

Lord Ellenborough would rather perhaps be remembered for his own successful averting of a threat to his gastronomic preferences. He had a sensible passion for turbot served with lobster sauce. When an application came before him for the release of men employed to collect lobsters in rock-pools from being pressed into the Royal Navy, he was horrified to discover that under recent legislation only deep-sea fishermen were free from this violent form of conscription. He struck a blow for the broad construction of the law and gave the men their liberty. He said, 'Is not the lobster-fishery a fishery, and a most important fishery, of this kingdom, though carried on in shallow water? The framers of the law well knew that the produce of the deep sea, without the produce of the shallow water, would be of comparatively small value, and intended that the turbot, when placed upon our tables, should be flanked by good lobster sauce.'

5. The Hammersmith Ghost and the Chelsea Set 1803 – 1878

In late 1803 the citizens of Hammersmith were perturbed by the ghost of a man who had recently cut his throat. A pregnant woman saw the white figure among the grave-stones, and died of fear. A waggoner saw the horrid creature with its long horns and glass eyes, and fled from his eight horses and sixteen passengers, leaving them 'in the greatest danger'. From the churchyard to the Malls and the Terrace no one would move at night unarmed.

Mr Thomas Millwood was a bricklayer and wore 'the usual habiliments of his occupation', long white trousers and a high white waistcoat. On the evening of 3 January 1804, he visited his father and sister near Black Lion Lane, and on hearing the watchman call the hour, he came out to return home to his wife. Francis Smith was an exciseman, honest and popular nevertheless. He and his friend, Mr Girdler, the watchman, were determined to dispose of the ghost; and Mr Smith, with a gun, and Mr Girdler with a pistol, roamed the alleyways. It was a dark night, and as Mr Millwood walked between two high hedges in Black Lion Lane, Mr Smith challenged him, got no answer, and shot him dead. When he saw what he had done, Mr Smith was appalled. He surrendered himself to a passing wine merchant, and Mr Girdler took them both to the comfort of the Black Lion to await the law.

Mr Smith did not have to wait long. Ten days later, he stood in the dock before the Lord Chief Baron and the judges of the Old Bailey, charged with murder. The wine-merchant, the watchman, the bricklayer's sister gave their evidence. Before 1898 the prisoner could not give sworn evidence on his own

Many witnesses were called . . . to speak of the alarming reputation of the ghost.

behalf, but he made a short statement from the dock; that he had had good intentions and had not known what he was doing. Many witnesses were called by his counsel to speak of the alarming reputation of the ghost, and of the prisoner's 'humane generous and benevolent disposition'. The public was on the prisoner's side. It is recorded that the great Mr Dignum of Drury Lane Theatre, that celebrated singer of 'No Song, No Supper', sat beside the prisoner and suffered with him 'the greatest agitation'.

The Lord Chief Baron then directed the jury. If they were satisfied the prisoner killed Mr Millwood, and shot him intentionally, it was murder. There was no issue, he said, of provocation or self-defence, which could reduce the charge. The fact that he did not know Mr Millwood or bear any spite against him was irrelevant. Rather curiously, he ignored the possibility that the prisoner might have thought he was shooting a ghost and not a man at all, but the summing-up was brisk and intelligible, and like many such summings-up it met with an odd answer. After an hour and a quarter the jury returned a verdict of manslaughter. All four judges then lectured the jury upon the law: it was murder, they said, or nothing. The jury conferred with each other and returned another verdict: guilty of murder. The Lord Chief Baron said the case would be reported to His Majesty immediately, and the Recorder then passed sentence of death on the prisoner in the usual form, which was 'that he should be executed on Monday next, and his body given to the surgeons to be dissected'. But a respite arrived at the Old Bailey before seven o'clock, and Mr Smith ended up with a year's imprisonment. There are still bricklayers in Black Lion Lane, but for fear of a similar disaster, they do not wear the habiliments of their occupation.

In the summer of 1803 William Blake was feeling tetchy. After three years the magic of cottage life in rural Sussex had faded. His wife found it rheumatic. His patron, Mr Hayley, who had brought him down from London to make engravings for him, was exasperating. 'Mr H', Blake wrote, 'approves of My Designs as little as he does of my Poems . . . I am determin'd to be no longer Pester'd with his Genteel Ignorance and Polite Disapprobation. I know myself both Poet and Painter.' Approaching fifty, he did indeed know this, but by reason of his rarefied methods of book production, his incompetence at public relations, and the modernity of his genius, no one else very much knew it, and he was not soothed by fame or money.

So when one morning he went out into his garden and there found a soldier talking to William, his gardener, Blake ordered the soldier out and firmly marched him some fifty yards down the road to the Fox Inn, where the man was billeted. Private Scolfield, the soldier, had a friend there, Private Cock. They felt their dignity at stake, and the result was a written complaint signed by Scolfield to the magistrate, that Blake, 'a miniature painter', had uttered seditious expressions. There is a long list of these expressions allegedly uttered in the garden, some more coherent than others, a description of the forced walk to the Fox, and then: 'at the same time Blake damned the King and said the — soldiers were all slaves'. The last expression could be 'proved' by another soldier, meaning Private Cock.

At the beginning of the nineteenth century there was grave doubt among lawyers as to whether you needed two witnesses for the prosecution to prove the terrible felony of treason, or whether one would do. Of old the eminent jurist Coke had said one thing, the learned Hale another. The Act of 1795 had laid down that it must be two. The Act of 1800 said that in all cases of high treason a man should be tried in all respects and on like evidence as if he were charged with murder, where one witness was enough. So the evidence of Private Cock, who had not been in the garden, was felt to be vital, the matter of law being in doubt.

. . . whatever unlawful words Blake used were said in heat in his garden . . .

This put the prosecution, if there were to be one, in a spot. There had been no one present in the garden, save Scolfield and Blake, Mrs Blake, and William the gardener, who was also ostler at the Fox. Mrs Blake was not a possible witness against her husband. William was on good terms with his employer. At the Fox there were many witnesses to the arrival of Scolfield. Mr Grinder, the landlord, was there with his wife and daughter, also Mrs Haynes, Blake's next-door neighbour, and her daughter, Mr Hayley's gardener, and Private Cock. It seemed, and seems, very much more likely that whatever unlawful words Blake used were said in heat in his garden and not in front of the village at the Fox. Indeed the written complaint supports this. But Private Cock, it was decided, must be called to support Private Scolfield, and that meant proving that the words were spoken at the Fox and not in Blake's garden.

Blake was committed for trial at the quarter sessions to be held at Chichester, but not, after all, on a charge of treason. He was indicted and tried for a lesser offence, sedition, for which the punishment was a fine and imprisonment, and not the horrid forms of death and torture reserved for treason. Two witnesses were not needed for this, but Private Cock was nonetheless ready to give his evidence, and the prosecution moved the scene of the crime accordingly.

The trial took place that winter at the ancient Guildhall. The Chairman of Quarter Sessions, the third Duke of Richmond, had in his youth demanded universal suffrage, annual general elections and recognition of the American rebels, but, approaching seventy, he had been tamed, and although disgruntled at lack of promotion by successive governments, he was against all reformers and radicals. Mr Hayley was unaware of Blake's view of him, and stood firmly by him. He had retained in Blake's defence a barrister, Samuel Rose, selected by him for the somewhat unusual reason that he had been a literary adviser and friend to the late William Cowper.

A prisoner could not then give evidence on his own behalf, but had to rely on the eloquence of counsel and on any supporting witnesses. This technicality did not prevent William

Blake, as the evidence of Scolfield and Cock progressed, from calling out 'Liar' – to the irritation of the Duke and the admiration of Mrs Blake. In fact, the evidence of the two soldiers went quite well for Blake, for Scolfield honestly limited himself to what had been said in the garden. The summary of Blake's words, according to Scolfield, amounted to his: 'If Bonaparte should come he would be Master of Europe in an hour's time, that England might depend upon it, that when he set his foot on English ground that every Englishman would have his choice whether to have his throat cut, or to join the French, and that he was a strong man, and would certainly begin to cut throats, and the strongest man must conquer – that he damned the King of England – his country and his subjects, that his soldiers were all bound for slaves, and all the poor people in general.' Cock could give evidence only as to what was said at the Fox.

Mr Rose opened the defence case in fine style. He had cross-examined Scolfield into an admission that he had formerly been a sergeant and was now reduced to the ranks for drunkenness. He kept his best point for the end of his speech. 'I would observe, in order to show that there is a small difference between the testimony of Cock and Scolfield – that when Scolfield was asked if anything had been uttered beside the words which were spoken in the garden, he replied no. Scolfield confines himself to the words in the garden – the other says they were uttered before the public house. If they were spoken in the garden the ostler must have heard them – if they were uttered before the public house Mrs Grinder must have heard them too. I will call these witnesses and you shall hear their account – you will then agree with me that they totally overthrow the testimony of these soldiers.'

Unfortunately, at this stage Mr Rose broke down and could speak no more. He was taken ill, and died within a matter of months. But for the purposes of the trial he had said enough. The village may not have understood or liked William Blake, but by January 1804 they were no longer in serious fear of invasion, and were tired of soldiers billeted on them at their expense. The gardener refused to support Scolfield, the others did not support Cock. The Duke nevertheless summed up with an invitation to the jury to convict. He would have summed up a great deal more fiercely if he had had any notion of what the literary historians now refer to as the seditious writings of Blake, composed but not widely published in the 1790s. 'Everybody hates a king', he had written in the margin of Bacon's *Essays*.

The jury, also not readers of the poet, acquitted Blake, and Mr Hayley went straight up to the Duke outside.

HAYLEY: I congratulate Your Grace, that after having been wearied with the condemnation of sorry vagrants, you have at last had the gratification of seeing an honest man honorably delivered from an infamous persecution. Mr Blake is a pacific, industrious and deserving artist.

THE DUKE (rather impolitely, reports Hayley): I know nothing of him.

HAYLEY: True, My Lord, Your Grace can know nothing of him; and I have therefore given you this information: I wish Your Grace a good Night.

The acquittal, right or wrong, of Blake was a success, but the charge and the wait and the trial were a real disaster for him. For the rest of his life he believed that there had been a conspiracy among the powerful to convict him. Scolfield (but not Cock as far as I know) under various spellings appears as a villain in his later writings. He ceased to be tetchy, but became exceedingly disillusioned, and exceedingly wary of writing about politics.

Supervision following imprisonment is part of the penal machinery of today, but the Regency had its own methods.

When at twenty-one the Marquess of Sligo inherited his father's title and fortune, England was deep in the Napoleonic wars, but this did not deter him from a splendid jaunt in his yacht. He visited Greece, and took away a fine haul of ancient ornaments and statues, together with two Albanians armed with silver-stocked pistols and silver daggers. He harboured his yacht in the summer of 1810 at Gibraltar, where some of his crew disappeared. He promptly persuaded two British sailors to desert their warship and join him. When asked about the missing men, young Lord Sligo denied that the men were on his yacht. Eventually they left it. He sailed on happily to Zante, and then, with Lady Hester Stanhope, the passionate Bonapartist and explorer, and her lover, Michael Bruce, he toured the Greek islands, hobnobbed with Byron and wintered in Constantinople and Asia Minor. Loaded with more silks and statues, he then sailed home, commissioned by Lady Hester to explain some features of her private life to her English connections.

The antique vases and bas reliefs were duly unloaded. He had had his bed unstuffed and the silks sewn in. He sailed through customs, losing nothing to them but a pair of embroidered slippers. Confident that he would be able to handle Lady Hester's connections in the same style, he proceeded towards London. But while he had been travelling, the navy had reported his activities in Gibraltar, and Lord Sligo to his horror was sent to be tried at the Old Bailey for enticing British sailors from their duty in time of war.

The trial took place in December 1812. The Lord Chief Justice, Lord Ellenborough, presided, and sat with Sir William Scott, the most earnest and scholarly maritime judge of the age. The trial was extremely short and hardly worth the application of such great learning, but not a moment of it was missed by the Dowager Marchioness of Sligo, whose pleas on behalf of her son would, it was hoped, soften the heart of the august Sir William. His heart was indeed softened; but not towards Lord Sligo, upon whom he pronounced the sentence of four months in Newgate and a fine of £5,000. While Lord

68

... when he came out of prison he found he had to acknowledge as step-father the man who had treated him so summarily.

Sligo was still serving his time, Sir William married the Dowager Marchioness, and when he came out of prison he found he had to acknowledge as stepfather the man who had treated him so summarily. It is not surprising that he immediately went abroad again. As to the Dowager Marchioness, Michael Bruce wrote:

'I was not a little surprised to hear of Lady Sligo's intended with Sir W. Scott. I should have thought that the old judge had suffered so much under the matrimonial yoke that he would have preferred living free during the remainder of his life... She is still what the French call *une veuve fringante*, a gamesome widow, and looks as if warm blood still flows in her veins.'

In the event the energetic Sir William soon exhausted his gamesome wife, who died only five years later, he himself living on into his nineties.

By the 1820s Mr Justice Graham had acquired a remarkable reputation at the Old Bailey for civility. Sixteen defendants awaited sentence, mostly for petty theft. Sir Henry Hawkins, himself a less polite judge, tells a story which illustrates the famous charm of Mr Justice Graham's manner.

'His Lordship, instead of reading the whole of the sixteen names, omitted one, and read only fifteen. He then politely, and with exquisite precision and solemnity, exhorted them severally to prepare for the awful doom that awaited them the following Monday, and pronounced on each the sentence of death. They left the dock. After they were gone the jailer explained to his Lordship that there had been sixteen prisoners capitally convicted, but that his Lordship had omitted the name of one of them, and he would like to know what was to be done with him. Mr Justice Graham: "What is the prisoner's name?" Jailer: "John Robins, My Lord." Mr Justice Graham: "Oh, bring John Robins back – by all means let John Robins step forward. I am obliged to you. John Robins, I find I have accidentally omitted your name in my list of prisoners doomed to execution. It was quite accidental, I assure you, and I ask your pardon for my mistake. I am very sorry, and can only add that you will be hanged with the rest."

Sir Henry Hawkins, Lord Brampton, may have thought Mr Justice Graham a trifle eccentric, but here he records a typical after-dinner trial of the 1840s at the Old Bailey.

PROSECUTION COUNSEL: I think you were walking up Ludgate Hill on Thursday, twenty-fifth, about half-past two in the afternoon, and suddenly felt a tug at your pocket and missed your handkerchief, which the constable now produces. Is that it?

WITNESS: Yes, sir.

JUDGE TO DEFENDANT: I suppose you have nothing to ask him? Next witness.

PROSECUTION COUNSEL: Were you following the prosecutor on the occasion when he was robbed on Ludgate Hill? And did you see the prisoner put his hand into the prosecutor's pocket and take this handkerchief out of it?

CONSTABLE: Yes, sir.

JUDGE TO DEFENDANT: Nothing to say, I suppose?

JUDGE TO JURY: Gentlemen, I suppose you have no doubt? I have none.

JURY: Guilty, My Lord.

JUDGE TO DEFENDANT: Jones, we have met before – we shall not meet again for some time – seven years' transportation. Next case.

This, Sir Henry said, took two minutes fifty-three seconds. After-dinner trials did not occupy an average of more than four minutes each. The grander judges dined at five, the regular Old Bailey ones at six. The chaplain of Newgate, a busy man, dined twice nightly.

If Dick Francis ever feels like a jaunt into the past, I would suggest the Derby of 1844. The favourite, Ratan, was mysteriously poisoned in his stable just before the race. A near favourite, Leander, was put out early in the race by a kick from Running Rein, who went on to win. Leander was destroyed, buried, dug up, proved to be a four-year-old and for that reason ineligible to run. Colonel Peel, the owner of Orlando, who came second, claimed the stake-money, on the basis that the horse which came first was yet another four-year-old, substituted for the true Running Rein. The Jockey Club suspended all bets. The court froze the stake money. Mr Wood, owner of Running Rein, sued Colonel Peel, and the action was tried at Westminster by Mr Baron Alderson, an experienced judge of horses.

Cockburn, later Lord Chief Justice, appeared for the Plaintiff, Mr Wood and called a line of witnesses who purported to give a full history of Running Rein from birth to winning-post. Colonel Peel, he said, was simply a respectable front-man for a conspiracy of society gamblers.

THE JUDGE (suddenly): Is the horse here?
COLONEL PEEL'S COUNSEL: Though we obtained an order from Your Lordship for inspection of the horse, we have been refused permission to inspect it.
COCKBURN: We refused because the manner in which inspection was demanded was improper.

72

JUDGE: There may be a good reason for the refusal, but it will only be overlooked if the horse is produced now. I should like to see it myself. I should like to look at his mouth.

COCKBURN: Of course, My Lord, there will be no objection.

The court adjourned. Late in the afternoon, William Smith, the trainer of Running Rein, came to the box to give his evidence for Mr Wood.

JUDGE: Is the horse in your possession now?

SMITH: No it's not.

JUDGE: Where is it?

SMITH: It was fetched away from me last Wednesday.

JUDGE: By whom?

SMITH: I had a verbal order from Mr Wood to deliver it over to a man who called for it.

JUDGE: And so you gave up this horse to a man who came to claim it, without any written order from Mr Wood?

SMITH: I thought –

JUDGE: No, no. I see the drift of it. This was the very day before my order reached the place – an order that was contemptuously disobeyed.

SMITH: When Your Lordship's order was read to me, I said that, if they required, I would go to Mr Wood and get his authority to hand over the horse.

JUDGE: When the horse had been taken away, and you had no idea where, why didn't you say you hadn't got the horse?

SMITH: I wasn't asked the question.

JUDGE: I don't believe you, sir. The horse was sent away in anticipation of my order. It was a gross contempt of court for which you will have to answer.

COCKBURN: My Lord, there will surely be time enough to discuss that when –

JUDGE: No doubt. It seems to me that justice demands the production of this horse.

COCKBURN: There will be no objection, My Lord. But my witnesses have proved identity.

JUDGE: Let us have the advantage of seeing it.

COCKBURN: I regret that this has made so great an impression on Your Lordship's mind. If only –

JUDGE: I will tell you what has made this great impression on my mind: that is your anxiety to conceal this horse.

COCKBURN: But My Lord –

JUDGE: Produce the horse. Produce the horse – that is the best answer to the question.

Two days passed. Horseless witnesses came and went. Next morning Cockburn called no witness.

COCKBURN: My Lord, after what fell from Your Lordship yesterday, I feel extreme difficulty in attempting to proceed without producing Running Rein for the court's inspection.

JUDGE: It is the only course to pursue.

COCKBURN: Then, My Lord, I am left without any course at all. Last night, when my client went to his stables, he found that Running Rein had been taken away, without his sanction and against his will.

JUDGE: A clear case of horse-stealing. If I ever try the parties who removed him, I will transport them for a certainty.

Colonel Peel took his verdict and the stake-money for the winner. But the spirit of the judge who insisted on inspection still reverberates: produce the horse.

Barthélemy, a French radical who had shot down a Paris policeman in very cold blood and without much reason, came to England in 1852, fell out with a fellow emigré, and killed him in a duel near Windsor. 'Everything about the duel was absurd,' says Herzen: 'they fought near Windsor, to do which they had to go by train (which goes only to Windsor) some

74

. . . only permits himself at the most absurd or critical moments to blow his nose . . .

dozens of miles away from the frontier into the heart of the kingdom, whereas people usually fight duels near the frontier, close to ships, boats and so on.' Windsor, naturally, was always well policed. 'I suppose that this place was chosen very simply because of all the environs of London the French knew only two: Richemon' and Vinsour.' When the survivors alighted at Waterloo Station, bearded, in foreign caps, and carrying wrapped-up rapiers, they were promptly arrested.

Herzen the keenest of European observers, was watching the Lord Chief Justice at work at the Surrey Assizes. It was the first time he had seen an English Court.

'Old Lord Campbell, who had grown grey and wrinkled in his judicial armchair, reading in an impassive voice with a Scotch accent the most frightening evidences, and unravelling the most complex cases with palpable clarity – he was to be out-witted by a handful of Parisian clubistes! ... Lord Campbell, who never raises his voice, never loses his temper, never smiles, and only permits himself at the most absurd or critical moments to blow his nose ... Lord Campbell with the face of a peevish old woman, in which if you look intently you can clearly discern the celebrated metamorphosis that so unpleas-antly surprised Little Red Riding Hood; you see that it is not grandmamma at all, but a wolf in a wig, a woman's dressing-gown and a fur-trimmed jacket.'

Barthélemy and the seconds at the duel were duly convicted, but Lord Campbell, pitying the ignorant foreigners, sentenced them to a mere two months imprisonment apiece.

Barthélemy was soon back before him. In late 1854 he murdered both a small tradesman and the policeman who tried to arrest him. The English press was shocked that he had not been hanged before. Herzen tells us that the Frenchman's lawyer, Mr Hering, visited him in prison on the eve of ex-ecution.

BARTHÉLEMY: I have nothing: I cannot repay your trouble with anything but my gratitude. I should have liked at least to leave you something for a keepsake, but I have nothing I could offer you. Perhaps my overcoat?

HERING: I shall be very grateful to you, very: I had wanted to ask you for it.

BARTHÉLEMY: With the greatest pleasure, but it is a wretched thing.

HERING: Oh, I am not going to wear it; I confess to you frankly, I have already sold it, and very well too.

BARTHÉLEMY: Sold it?

HERING: Yes, to Madame Tussaud for her gallery.

When Barthélemy was being taken to be hanged, he suddenly said to the sheriff: 'Oh, I quite forgot to ask you: *on no account* let my overcoat be given to Hering.'

First briefs are always alarming, but few draw so much public attention as the following, which was delivered in 1863.

Mrs Briggs had instructed her counsel that she was in the omnibus, a hymn book in her pocket, on her way to tea and prayers, when she was seized and monstrously accused of having just picked someone's pocket. The purse found on her must have been planted by some evil worldling. Counsel was holding his first brief and, determined to draw attention to the hymn-book, cross-examined the policeman with all the assurance he could muster.

GILBERT: You say you found the purse in her pocket, my man?

CONSTABLE: Yes, sir.

GILBERT: Did you find anything else?

CONSTABLE: Yes, sir.

GILBERT: What?

CONSTABLE: Two other purses, a watch with the bow

broken, three handkerchiefs, two silver pencil-cases, and a hymn-book.

Before Mrs Briggs went below to start her eighteen-month sentence, she paused briefly to remove her boot and hurl it at her counsel, W. S. Gilbert (for it was he). 'The language in which her ovation was couched was perfectly shocking,' he noted soon afterwards. 'The boot missed me, but hit a reporter on the head, and to this fact I am disposed to attribute the unfavourable light in which my search for the defence was placed in two or three leading daily papers next morning.'

Gilbert practised at the bar for four years, with an average of five clients a year, and earned £75. Happily it was not long before he found more lucrative employment through meeting Arthur Sullivan in 1871.

London in 1869 had a gutter press, of which the most scurrilous journal was the *Queen's Messenger*. Its articles appeared anonymously. The very editor was unknown, and no one could sue it for libel. The *Queen's Messenger* took against the young Lord Carrington, or at any rate against his family, of whom his ancestor, a banker, had been created a peer in 1796. The result was a snobbish tirade in their most felicitous manner. 'To take a bargaining bumpkin, with his pedlar's nature, and give to the rogue two coronets in one year is an outrage upon decency. What can possibly be expected of such a stock except a progeny of lackeys? The very souls of such knaves are crushed out of shape by the load of honour laid on them.'

Lord Carrington made some enquiries and discovered a Mr Grenville Murray of the Conservative Club, and of Albany, as the principal Mr Puff of the paper. He looked at a photograph of Mr Murray, waited outside the Club, and when Mr Murray emerged, whipped him soundly then told him who he was. Mr Murray, supported by the club porter, laid an information against Lord Carrington for assault Lord Carrington pleaded not guilty so as to force Mr Murray to give evidence on oath. Before the magistrate Mr Murray swore that he had no connection with the *Queen's Messenger* at all, and the defendant was committed for trial. Lord Carrington was undaunted. He charged Mr Murray with perjury in the evidence he had given before the magistrate and got him committed also for trial. He retained as his counsel the quiet but persistent Sir John Coleridge. You can hear the very quietness of Sir John as cross-examination developed.

COLERIDGE: Have you ever written in the *Queen's Messenger*?

MURRAY: I am advised to decline answering any questions about the *Queen's Messenger*.

COLERIDGE: Why do you decline?

MURRAY: Because they are trying to convict me of perjury – on stolen evidence.

COLERIDGE: On what ground have you been advised not to answer? You have no right to refuse, you know – except on the ground that it would incriminate you. Do you believe it would expose you to criminal consequences?

MURRAY: I don't know.

COLERIDGE: I am asking you whether you have ever written in the *Queen's Messenger* – and it is your duty to answer unless it would incriminate you.

MURRAY: I have come to see what a poor man can do against a rich one.

COLERIDGE: It is a very simple question. Do you know the *Queen's Messenger*?

MURRAY: I decline to answer.

COLERIDGE: Do you fear to answer?

MURRAY: Unquestionably I do. How can I not fear when there is so much money against me, while I have not a shilling?

COLERIDGE: After you had admitted your identity, didn't Lord Carrington say to you, 'You have written against my family in your paper?'

MURRAY: I think he did something of the kind.

COLERIDGE: Did you know what he meant?

MURRAY: I had a vague knowledge.

COLERIDGE: What did you think he meant?

MURRAY: You wish to get me round to the old ground. I stand here as the representative of the press, and you shall know nothing about it from me.

COLERIDGE: What paper did you understand Lord Carrington to mean when he said 'your paper'?

MURRAY: How was I to know?

COLERIDGE: I thought you had vague knowledge.

MURRAY: Vague knowledge is not evidence.

COLERIDGE: Had you any idea what he meant?

MURRAY: I decline to answer.

COLERIDGE: Did you believe that it had anything to do with the *Queen's Messenger*?

MURRAY: My belief is not evidence either.

COLERIDGE: Have you seen the *Queen's Messenger* placarded all over London?

MURRAY: Yes.

COLERIDGE: Do you read it?

MURRAY: Yes.

COLERIDGE: Do you like it?

No answer, but laughter in court. The jury convicted: they had no alternative. The judge bound over Lord Carrington to keep the peace, and Mr Grenville Murray broke his own bail and fled.

Sir James Ingham at the age of seventy-one became Chief Metropolitan Magistrate in London, and he sat daily in that demanding office until he died at the age of eighty-five. One day he had before him at Bow Street two angry men. The complainant had been travelling on the old South Western railway from Bournemouth to London. There were no corridors to the carriages and he travelled alone to Basingstoke, where the defendant came into his compartment. The complainant dozed until Vauxhall, woke up, felt across his waistcoat and found his watch and chain were missing. The defendant was reading the newspaper.

COMPLAINANT: Has any one else entered this compartment while I have been asleep?
DEFENDANT: No.
COMPLAINANT: Then, sir, I must request you to tell me what you have done with my watch. It has been stolen during the time that you have been in the carriage. You had better return it, or I shall have to give you in charge on our arrival at Waterloo.

The defendant was indignant, but at Waterloo a porter was sent to fetch a constable and the defendant was brought at once before Sir James, who asked the complainant if he had seen any other man come near the defendant at Waterloo.

COMPLAINANT: Yes, another man came up, apparently to enquire what was the matter.
SIR JAMES: Just so. That accounts for the disappearance of the watch. These things are never done alone – wherever a theft takes place, whether in a train, a crowd, or elsewhere, there is always a confederate to receive the stolen property. Prisoner, you are remanded for a week; but if you are a respectable man, I have no objection to take very substantial bail.

The defendant's indignation burst out. He had just come home from years of foreign travel, he could find no friend to put up bail, he was being imprisoned without trial. Sir James was prevailed on to hear the case next day.

In the morning it was the complainant, and not the defendant, who spoke.

COMPLAINANT : I do not know how to express my regret for what has occurred. I find I did not lose my watch after all. I communicated my loss by telegraph to my wife at Bournemouth, and she has written to say that my watch and chain are safe at home. I dressed hurriedly to catch my train. I must have entirely forgotten to take my watch from the dressing-table.

Sir James's wisdom was adaptable to the new facts. He had not spent the night in jail.

SIR JAMES : It is a most remarkable occurrence. To show, however, how liable we all are to make these mistakes, I may mention, as an extraordinary coincidence, that I myself have only this morning been guilty of precisely the same oversight. I was under the impression, when I left my house at Kensington, that I put my watch (which, I may mention, is an exceedingly valuable one) in my pocket; but on arriving at this court, I found that I must have left it at home by mistake.

The defendant was discharged amid much apologizing from the complainant, much worldly smiling from the bench, although Sir James was less amused to find that the prisoner in the next case was absent. He completed his day's work and returned to Kensington, where his daughter met him in the drawing-room.

MISS INGHAM : Papa, dear, I suppose you got your watch all right ?
SIR JAMES : Well, my dear, as a matter of fact I went out this morning without it.
MISS INGHAM : Yes, I know, papa, but I gave it to the man from Bow Street who called for it.

James McNeill Whistler could seldom resist a tussle in the courts if an opportunity arose. When in 1878 Ruskin wrote, 'I have seen, and heard, much of cockney impudence before now ; but never expected to hear a coxcomb ask two hundred guineas for flinging a pot of paint in the public's face,' Whistler immediately took action.

SIR JOHN HOLKER, Attorney-General: Did it take much time to paint the 'Nocturne in Black and Gold' ? How soon did you knock it off ?

WHISTLER: I beg your pardon ?

ATTORNEY-GENERAL :   I was using an expression which was rather more applicable to my own profession. How long did you take to knock off one of your pictures ?

WHISTLER: Oh, I 'knock off' one possibly in a couple of days – one day to do the work and another to finish it.

ATTORNEY-GENERAL :   And that was the labour for which you asked two hundred guineas ?

WHISTLER: No, it was for the knowledge gained through a lifetime.

Judgment for the plaintiff, Whistler, against the defendant, Ruskin, for one farthing. No order for costs.

Some six years later, by then living in Paris, Whistler thought he would have a go in the French courts. His protagonist was Sir William Eden, who had wanted a portrait of his wife. Whistler's London agents had asked for 500 guineas. Sir William rejected this proposal and negotiated through George Moore, the critic, for a slighter work, watercolour perhaps, for 100 or 150 guineas. Lady Eden was beautiful and agreeable and Whistler enjoyed painting her. He produced a full-length portrait in oil, much admired, as it proceeded, by the Edens.

On 14 February 1894 the picture being more or less complete, Sir William handed Whistler an envelope and told him to open it later. In it Whistler found a cheque for 100 guineas and a note.

'Dear Mr Whistler – Herewith your Valentine-cheque value one hundred guineas. The picture will always be of inestimable value to me, and will be handed down as an heirloom so long as heirlooms last! I shall always look with pleasure to the painting of it – and, with thanks, remain yours sincerely, William Eden.'

Whistler replied the same day with a note almost as ambiguous in its English as in its later French translation when read out in the French court.

'My dear Sir William – I have your valentine. You really are magnificent – and have scored all round. I can only hope that the little picture will prove even slightly worthy of all of us, and I rely on Lady Eden's amiable promise to let me add the few last touches we know of. She has been so courageous and kind all along in doing her part. With best wishes again for your journey, very faithfully J. McNeill Whistler.'

Puzzled somewhat by the note, Sir William called next day. He found the artist at the foot of his stairs and furious at receiving a mere hundred guineas for his work. Whistler proposed a duel. Sir William proposed the figure at the top of the agreed bracket, 150 guineas. Both offers were rejected, and Sir William departed to shoot tigers in India.

Whistler then sent the picture for exhibition at the Champ de Mars in Paris, where 'Brown and gold, Portrait of Lady E' was a resounding success. When he returned to England at the end of the year, Sir William demanded delivery of the picture. Whistler refused. Sir William issued a summons through the French Courts demanding it. Whistler again refused, though through his lawyers he repaid the hundred guineas. Then he attacked the painting. He wiped out the fair face of Lady Eden, and, at the request of another customer, Mr Hale, replaced it with the face of Mrs Hale. It was a challenge, and it was met.

Sir William sued before the appropriate court, the Civil

Tribunal of the Seine, and triumphed. The court held that he was entitled to the picture, to the hundred guineas, interest, costs and £40 damages. Whistler appealed. His barrister argued formidably. Surely Sir William could not have both his money back and the picture? Why should he be entitled to a portrait which was of Mrs Hale? He might be entitled to his money back, but why to damages? His client was concerned with honour, not money. Sir William was shown to be a dealer, someone who would sell his pictures for profit, even those depicting his family. He was mean and a materialist, and the artist had kept the picture properly to expose him.

The appeal court decided that the much-mutilated work should remain with Whistler. It had been a contract to paint a portrait, and it had not been finished, as Whistler's note to Sir William stated. But Whistler was forbidden to exhibit it again, and should hand it over to Sir William when he, the artist, thought it was complete. The damages, interest and costs should stand, although Sir William had to pay the costs of the appeal.

Out of this messy story Whistler constructed an elegant little book, *Eden Versus Whistler, the Baronet and the Butterfly, a Valentine With a Verdict*, drawing a toad for the baronet, and a butterfly as usual for himself. He had established, he claimed, 'the Absolute Right of the Artist to control the destiny of his handiwork – and, at all times, and in all circumstances, to refuse its delivery into unseemly and ridiculous keeping'. Although it was a clever little book its obvious bitterness, rather than the trial, brought down ridicule upon Whistler.

6. Women and Children Second 1878 – 1884

In 1925 Parliament enacted that in all cases concerning children the court should regard the welfare of the child and not the claims of the parents as the paramount consideration. It was a quieter revolution than the giving of the vote to women six years earlier, but no less important.

Back in 1863 the Honourable Leopold Agar-Ellis, a member of the Church of England, had paid his addresses to the Honourable Harriet Stonor, daughter of Lord Camoys, of an old Catholic family. Trouble was resolved at the house of the Duke of Sutherland, where in the presence of the Duke and Lord Camoys, the parties solemnly agreed that their wedding should be celebrated in both churches and any children should be brought up as Catholics. Of the marriage, three children survived, Caroline, Harriet and Evelyn Mary. The father went back on his promise. He had the children baptised in the Church of England and looked after by Protestant nurses and governesses. The mother had them baptised as Catholics, and taught them Catholic prayers. It was not until the children got together and refused to go to the Protestant church that the father really woke up to what was happening. There were furious scenes. He got in first with the law, had the children made wards of court, and applied to the court for directions for their education and upbringing, proposing to board them with a Protestant clergyman. The mother petitioned for directions that they should stay in her care and as Catholics. They were settled, she said, and any other course could be unfair on them. Caroline was twelve, Harriet eleven, and Evelyn Mary nine.

On 5 August 1878 Vice-Chancellor Malins gave his judgment, slipping at once into the heavy rhythm which beats through all the judgments. He repeated the whole story including the solemn agreement before the marriage:

'This is perhaps the strangest case that has ever occurred showing the misery that ensues from mixed marriages ... Mrs Agar-Ellis is a lady of education; she says she has educated her children with the greatest care, and I am satisfied she has done so, and Mr Agar-Ellis, I am sure, entirely acquiesces in that view of the case. But it is evident that from the year 1865 down to the presentation of this petition this struggle has been going on, the father desiring the children to be brought up as Protestants, and the mother determined that they should be brought up as Roman Catholics, and taking advantage of every opportunity she had to instruct them in doctrines of the Roman Catholic church, and to bring them up in every way she could as Roman Catholics; and I am very sorry to find that she has thought herself justified in going to such an extent as this, that she has set at defiance the authority of the father over the children, and has so far instilled these principles into the children; and I cannot but express my regret that she has done so, seeming to have entirely forgotten that by the laws of England, by the laws of Christianity, and by the constitution of society, when there is a difference between husband and wife, it is the duty of the wife to submit to the husband ... The principles of this court are the principles of common sense and the principles of propriety, that the children must be brought up in the religion of the father. The father is the head of the house, he must have the control of his family, he must say how and by whom they are to be educated, and where they are to be educated, and this court never does interfere between a father and his children unless there be an abandonment of the parental duty.'

The Vice-Chancellor went on to show that he was no religious bigot, and he cited an Irish case.

'Lord O'Hagan is a judge for whom I entertain the greatest possible respect. He is a Roman Catholic, as we all know, and

. . . when there is a difference between husband and wife, it is the duty of the wife to submit . . .

he had here to decide whether the children should be brought up in the religion of the father, which was Protestant, or in the religion of the mother, which was Roman Catholic, and where there had been as positive an understanding on the part of the father as could be given, which was not in controversy. Now Lord O'Hagan, on the subject of the duty of the father, expresses it thus, and every word of this is applicable to the present case: "The authority of a father to guide and govern the education of his child is a very sacred thing, bestowed by the Almighty, and to be sustained to the uttermost by human law. It is not to be abrogated or abridged, without the most coercive reason. For the parent and the child alike, its mainten-ance is essential, that their reciprocal relations may be fruitful of happiness and virtue; and no disturbing intervention should be allowed between them, whilst those relations are pure and wholesome and conducive to their mutual benefit." Lord O'Hagan came to the conclusion that it was his duty to have the children brought up, not in the religion of the mother, but of the father... I came to the conclusion in this case that the father, however absolutely he may have promised, is at liberty to revoke it... I cannot interfere with the right of Mr Agar-Ellis to do as he pleases with his own children. I intend my judgment to leave him master of his own house.'

The mother appealed. Her counsel, Sir H.S.Giffard, later Lord Chancellor, did not find the going easy.

LORD JUSTICE BAGGALLAY: Suppose a boy said, 'I wish to go to sea'?

GIFFARD: The court would not allow its ward to do any thing improper; but suppose the ward a girl, and the father wished to bring her up for a ballet-dancer, would the court allow it?

Their Lordships did not respond to this astonishing sug-gestion.

GIFFARD: It is assumed on the other side that these children for years were brought up as Protestants, but the father must have been perfectly sure all along that they were receiving Roman Catholic instruction from their mother. The evidence shows that for two years there were scenes with them when their father took them to Protestant places of worship, and at last they refused to go. Now the court is asked to compel them to go whether they like it or not. Great danger of unsettling their religious views altogether will arise.

LORD JUSTICE JAMES: If the attempt to change a person's religious views is necessarily prejudicial to his moral and religious welfare, as tending to unsettle him, then all misionary efforts are wrong.

Lord Justice James gave the judgment of the court, first disposing of the husband's promise to let the children be brought up as Catholics:

'It was conceded by counsel and, in truth, it is a principle and authority settled so as to be beyond question or argument, that the ante-nuptial promise is, in point of law, absolutely void.... If a good and honest father, taking into his consideration the past teaching to which his children have been, in fact, subject, and the effect of that teaching on their minds, and the risk of unsettling their convictions, comes to the conclusion that it is right and for their welfare, temporal and spiritual, that he should take means to counteract that teaching, and undo its effect, he is by law the proper and sole judge of that, and we, as judges of the land, have no more right to sit in appeal from the conclusion which he has conscientiously and honestly arrived at than we should have to sit in appeal from his conclusion as to the particular church his children should attend, the particular sermons they should hear, or the particular religious books to be placed in their hands.'

There was a pause, one hopes, for breath, after this monumental sentence, and the peroration soon began. 'He ought to discard, and we have no doubt will discard, all thought of personal dignity or personal supremacy or of triumph in a personal struggle. The law trusts to him that he will, rising above all such petty feelings, have sole regard to what he conscientiously believes to be for the temporal and spiritual welfare of his children, and we, pronouncing what we deem the law to be, must leave the matter to his sense of parental duty and to his conscience.'

At once the father took the girls from their mother's care, allowed her to see them once a month and required all letters between them to be shown to him. When Harriet was sixteen, she wrote to Mr Justice Fry, of whom she was technically the ward, and begged now to be allowed to live with her mother and practise the Catholic religion. 'His Lordship', says the report, 'directed his Chief Clerk to see the solicitors of Mr and Mrs Agar-Ellis with a view to some amicable arrangement being made, and ultimately Mr Agar-Ellis made proposals under which Miss Harriet Agar-Ellis was to be allowed, subject to his control, to practise the Roman Catholic religion, to attend service at the Roman Catholic church on Sundays and festivals, to prepare herself for her first communion.'

Harriet wrote to her mother's solicitor.

'Dear Mr Hastings, I write again to ask you to apply to the judge for leave that I may spend my vacation with my mother, as you know for these last two years I have been moved about from place to place, and have only had part of one vacation with my mother, which the judge ordered. The people I am with now are very kind to me, but they want to go abroad in July and are unable to take me with them. Father has no place to take me to, and with one exception has never spent a vacation with us over four years. I am always among strangers. I am longing to see some of my relations. I know you will do what you can for me. Yours very truly, Harriet Agar-Ellis.'

The mother petitioned the court for leave to have Harriet with her for the summer holidays. The father opposed it, and Mr Justice Pearson supported the father, saying he could change his mind if he wished and the case was concluded by the previous decision, now five years back. The mother again appealed, her counsel arguing that the welfare of Harriet deserved some consideration and an intelligent girl of sixteen should not be fettered in this way. The argument grew sulky.

91

LORD JUSTICE BOWEN: According to your argument a young lady of sixteen who was stopped by her father from going to Gretna Green might bring an action for false imprisonment.

COUNSEL FOR THE FATHER: If Mr Agar-Ellis is not allowed to bring up his children in the way that he deems best, he desires to intimate most respectfully to the court that he will consider himself discharged from all legal or moral obligation to maintain his daughter.

COUNSEL FOR THE MOTHER: The court will now in every case consider what is for the benefit of its ward. We ask the court to see the young lady.

Their Lordships refused.

COUNSEL FOR THE MOTHER: Then if the father will really withdraw his maintenance, the mother is now in a position to maintain them and will undertake to do so.

But the three distinguished judges who heard the appeal were not going to allow it. 'If we were not in a court of law,' said Lord Justice Bowen, 'but in a court of critics capable of being moved by feelings of favour or disfavour, we might be tempted to comment, with more or less severity, upon the way in which, so far as we have heard the story, the father has exercised his parental right. But it seems to me the court must not allow itself to drift out of the proper course; the court must not be tempted to interfere with the natural order and course of family life, the very basis of which is the authority of the father.'

And under it the Agar-Ellis girls had to stay.

Miss Fortescue was not much older than the Agar-Ellis girls but came from what was then regarded as a less privileged rank of society, the acting profession.

She was as good as she was beautiful. When her father failed in business, she felt a duty to support her mother and sister. She went on the stage, and was beginning to succeed in the D'Oyly Carte Company. Then she met Lord Garmoyle. They fell in love, and she accepted his proposal.

Lord Garmoyle was no aristocrat by birth. His father, a great lawyer, had been created a baron in 1867, Lord Chancellor in 1868, and raised to an earldom in 1878. Earl Cairns was a philanthropist and a most lucid judge. But, having risen so high, he was most reluctant to let his heir marry an actress, and young Lord Garmoyle had to tell Miss Fortescue that his parents would not tolerate her shocking profession. His parents thought it frivolous, sinful and profane. Miss Fortescue humbly accepted their view and abandoned her career.

Lord Garmoyle was at Sandhurst and Miss Fortescue with her mother. They were now formally engaged, and Miss Fortescue was now accepted at the Earl's house. They exchanged loving letters. 'You know how ambitious I was for myself,' she wrote, 'Now my hopes are centred in and upon you. We shall be so happy.' She was preparing for another visit to the Earl and Countess when Lord Garmoyle put her off, saying his parents were not well. She went instead to Brighton with her mother, and Lord Garmoyle joined them, fond as ever. The night he left, he wrote her a letter. He retained, he wrote, the deepest love and admiration for her; thought her the finest and most wonderful of beings, but, looking to her profession, she would not be acceptable to his relatives and friends. 'Acting in the interests and on the suggestion of others' he had no choice but to break their engagement.

She had no choice but to sue for breach of promise of marriage. She had lost her career. Her mother was penniless. And when the case came to court in 1884 and she was offered the vast sum of £10,000 by way of damages, she had no option but to take it; though for this successful litigant her victory was as ashes, the whole business heart-breaking.

7. Sir Charles Russell and Adversaries 1885 – 1896

Mr William Thomas Stead was in 1885 the editor of the *Pall Mall Gazette*. His was a household name. He had been largely responsible for the despatch of General Gordon to Khartoum. He had strongly backed the Criminal Law Amendment Bill, then before Parliament, aimed at affording protection to women and children caught in the Victorian sexual underworld. The Bill was in trouble, and Mr Stead decided to show the public the ease with which a child could be sold into prostitution. He employed two women who had formerly plied this trade, and they bought Eliza Armstrong from her mother, talking of taking her away 'into service'. On Mr Stead's instructions she was kept under the protection of the Salvation Army and then taken for a holiday in France. No harm befell her; she remained intact; and Mr Stead used the material for an article in the *Gazette* he called 'A Child of Thirteen Bought for £5'.

Mrs Armstrong was shown the article. It mentioned no names, but she was thoroughly scared of exposure, and she went to the police. As a result, Mr Stead, the head of the Salvation Army, and others, were charged with abduction. Eliza was returned to her mother, although she appeared not very willing to do so. Sir Charles Russell, the famous and formidable advocate, was retained for Mr Stead.

Mrs Armstrong told the court how she had arranged for Eliza to go into service. No thought of anything else entered her head.

RUSSELL: When did you first become uneasy about your child?

MRS ARMSTRONG: When I got the *Pall Mall Gazette*.

RUSSELL: You don't ordinarily read the *Pall Mall Gazette*?

MRS ARMSTRONG: Never read it before or since.

RUSSELL: Neighbours called your attention to it?

MRS ARMSTRONG: Yes.

RUSSELL: Had you any anxiety before that?

MRS ARMSTRONG: Yes, because I hadn't heard of her.

RUSSELL: But you have just said you were first anxious when you saw the *Gazette*. Do you want to correct that answer?

MRS ARMSTRONG: Of course I do.

RUSSELL: Well, we will begin again. *When* did you first begin to be anxious?

MRS ARMSTRONG: About a fortnight after she'd gone.

RUSSELL: Did you enquire about her from Mrs Broughton?

MRS ARMSTRONG: Yes.

RUSSELL: What enquiry did you make?

MRS ARMSTRONG: Asked if she'd had any letter. She said no.

RUSSELL: That was as far as you went to ascertain where your child was?

ARMSTRONG: Yes.

RUSSELL: Did you know her address?

MRS ARMSTRONG: No.

RUSSELL: When she left, you didn't ask where she was going?

MRS ARMSTRONG: I thought Mrs Broughton knew all about it.

RUSSELL: Why didn't you ask Mrs Broughton for the address?

MRS ARMSTRONG: Didn't think it'd be any use. Mrs Jarrett had said her husband was a commercial traveller, so I didn't think they'd have any address.

RUSSELL: At any rate, you didn't ask Mrs Broughton for it?

MRS ARMSTRONG: Yes, I did.

RUSSELL: What, madam? Scarcely a moment ago you told

me you did not. Before the *Gazette*, had neighbours spoken to you about the disappearance of your child?

MRS ARMSTRONG: Two or three of them.

RUSSELL: Did some say you had sold her?

MRS ARMSTRONG: They said it seemed very much like it after the story in the *Gazette*.

RUSSELL: Didn't some of them say it before?

MRS ARMSTRONG: Yes, I suppose so.

RUSSELL: The *Gazette* article described how a child of thirteen was bought for £5?

MRS ARMSTRONG: Yes.

RUSSELL: But you hadn't sold your child for £5, had you?

MRS ARMSTRONG: No. But when Mrs Broughton admitted having a sovereign, I began to think there was something in it.

RUSSELL: You did? You've been in trouble once or twice, haven't you?

MRS ARMSTRONG: For what?

RUSSELL: Assault?

MRS ARMSTRONG: Years ago.

RUSSELL: Drunkenness?

MRS ARMSTRONG: Quite likely.

RUSSELL: On the very day Eliza left, weren't you taken up drunk in the street with your baby in your arms?

MRS ARMSTRONG: All through my husband. Knocking me about for letting Eliza go.

RUSSELL: Oh? If she had gone to genuine service, why should he knock you about?

MRS ARMSTRONG: I don't know.

RUSSELL: You had another daughter in service?

MRS ARMSTRONG: Yes.

RUSSELL: Did he knock you about on that occasion?

MRS ARMSTRONG: No.

It was a model cross-examination. The defendant was innocent of any indecent intention, but he was committed for trial, convicted and sentenced to three months' imprisonment, a genuine victim of the cant of the age. He survived long enough to drown in the *Titanic* in 1912.

Though not in the case of the well-meaning Mr Stead it was usually a disaster for the other side when Sir Charles Russell was retained. Campbell versus Campbell and Marlborough in 1886 was no exception. Lord Colin Campbell charged his wife with adultery with an eminent general, a fashionable physician, the head of the London Fire Brigade, and the Duke of Marlborough. Lady Colin retaliated with a housemaid, who proved to be a virgin, but she armed herself with Sir Charles. The trial lasted nineteen days. All really turned on the evidence of adultery by the wife with the Duke. They had been guests together at a country house. Lady Colin had slept in a double bed. Was it clear or true at all, as Rose Baer, Lady Colin's personal maid, asserted, that next morning there were the signs of two people having slept there? Rose had been sacked. Was she vindictive and unreliable?

RUSSELL: How long after you left Lady Colin's service did anyone connected with this case approach you?

BAER: I left in June 1882. And Lord Colin came to see me in December 1884.

RUSSELL: How did he know where to find you?

BAER: I don't know.

RUSSELL: Had you written to him?

BAER: No.

RUSSELL: Until December 1884, you had no communication with Lord Colin – or anyone on his behalf?

BAER: No.

RUSSELL: That is clear?

BAER: Yes.

Sir Charles Russell : So you agreed to give evidence without knowing what it was all about?
Rose Baer, lady's maid : Yes.

RUSSELL: When you saw Lord Colin, did you make a statement to him?

BAER: No. He just asked me if I would give evidence.

RUSSELL: Had you said up to that time that you could give evidence?

BAER: No.

RUSSELL: How did he know you could? Did you ask him how he knew?

BAER: No. I didn't.

RUSSELL: Did he say what the evidence was to be about?

BAER: No.

RUSSELL: Did you know what case you were to give evidence in?

BAER: No.

RUSSELL: Had you then heard of the divorce suits?

BAER: No.

RUSSELL: But when Lord Colin asked you to give evidence you agreed?

BAER: Yes.

RUSSELL: So you agreed to give evidence without knowing what it was all about?

BAER: Yes.

As usual Sir Charles' questions devastated, while they appeared so simple and inevitable. He followed them up with one of those pieces of personal rhetoric which the age adored, his final peroration a contrast in style to his cross-examination.

'I will make but a passing reference,' he said, 'to those parents, devoted and proud, already bent in age, and who will hereafter be bent in shame if your verdict will condemn their child. I make no appeal for mercy. I ask for justice, justice, justice, which forbids life or fame to be sacrificed save on evidence at once credible and cogent. Gentlemen, Lady Colin Campbell's life – nay, something dearer than life – is in your hands; and with an earnest heart and with a spirit of reverence I would humbly pray that your minds and your judgments be inclined to give in this case a just and honest deliverance.'

The jury was duly overwhelmed, and found Lady Colin and the Duke not guilty of adultery: so each side failed in its effort to end a hopeless marriage. Sir Charles' fees in that year came to £17,957.

Sir George Chetwynd, baronet, was a member of the Jockey Club, a leading owner, and a former steward. His principal jockey was the foremost in England, a man named Wood. Sir George did very well in his racing. In 1887 the third Earl of Durham, in the annual speech at the Gimcrack Club dinner, chose to speak about the corruption and decadence of the Turf. He spoke of 'owners who win large stakes when their horses are successful, but do not lose much when they are beaten', of 'a fashionable and aristocratic stable conspicuous throughout the season for the in-and-out running of its horses, which has disgusted the public and driven the handicapper to his wits' end to discover their true form', and of 'a notorious jockey known for his malpractices'. He did not name Chetwynd as the owner or Wood as the jockey, but his audience had little doubt.

Sir George may have been corrupt, but he was no coward. He asked the Earl bluntly if he had intended to refer to him. The Earl said he had. Sir George challenged him to a duel. The Earl rejected that challenge but gave the stewards of the Jockey Club a copy of his speech and wrote to them a letter accusing Sir George of being an accomplice in the pulling of his horses.

Sir George had no alternative: he sued for libel, and the Earl repeated his accusation and claimed he was justified in what he had said. The action was transferred by agreement to the three stewards of the Jockey Club, and before them came Sir Charles Russell as counsel for the Earl.

Chetwynd, like many before him, had something of a

mauling from Russell. The issue was how much Chetwynd knew of Wood's malpractices: and by the end of cross-examination it was apparent that Chetwynd knew more than he had admitted. Wood came next.

RUSSELL: Do you know a Mr Peel?

WOOD: Yes.

RUSSELL: Has he given you some handsome presents after races?

WOOD: Yes.

RUSSELL: Has he ever given you money when you were riding in a race and told him you thought some other horse would win?

WOOD: No.

RUSSELL: Will you swear that?

WOOD: I should think so.

RUSSELL: I put it to you as plainly as I can.

WOOD: Well, I might be riding in a race and he might ask me what I thought would win, and I might tell him.

RUSSELL: What is meant by a horse being out for an airing?

WOOD: It might mean that it's backward in condition.

RUSSELL: Not intended to win?

WOOD: No, backward in condition.

RUSSELL: What is meant by a horse being on the job?

WOOD: I suppose it means he's on the job.

RUSSELL: Have you ever ridden horses out for an airing?

WOOD: Dozens.

RUSSELL: Have you ever ridden a horse on the job?

WOOD: Every horse I've ridden has always been on the job.

RUSSELL: In the 1884 Cambridgeshire did you ride a horse called Sandiway?

WOOD: Yes.

RUSSELL: Was the race won by a mare called Florence owned by Mr Hammond?

WOOD: Yes.

RUSSELL: After the race did Mr Hammond give you £500?

WOOD: I don't know.

RUSSELL : Will you swear he didn't ?

WOOD : I can't swear.

RUSSELL : Have you any doubt that you did receive such a present ?

WOOD : I cannot say.

As Sir Charles' thunder overwhelmed Wood, Sir George's case collapsed. The stewards found that the Earl had been inaccurate in saying Sir George had told his jockey to pull – so he was entitled to nominal damages of a farthing – but they also found that Wood *had* pulled, and that Sir George had known about it. It was the end of Sir George Chetwynd's chances on the Turf.

The next year saw Sir Charles Russell's most celebrated performance, the cross-examination of Richard Pigott in 1888. It inspired Max Beerbohm to write the following paragraph :

'"Come, Mr Pigott", he is reported as saying at a crucial moment, "try to do yourself justice. Remember! You are face to face with my Lords." How well do I hear, in that awful hortation, Russell's pause after the word "Remember", and the lowered voice in which the subsequent words were uttered slowly, and the richness of solemnity that was given to the last word of all, ere the thin lips snapped together – those lips that were so significant a feature of that large, white, luminous and inauspicious face. It is an hortation which, by whomsoever delivered, would tend to dispirit the bravest and most honest of witnesses. The presence of a judge is always, as I have said, oppressive. The presence of three is trebly so. Yet not a score of them serried along the bench could have outdone in oppressiveness Sir Charles Russell.'

The previous year *The Times* had published a series of articles setting out to prove that Charles Parnell, the Irish leader, was a dangerous and formidable agitator. They then published a facsimile letter, purporting to be from Parnell himself, condoning the murder in Phoenix Park, Dublin of the Under-Secretary for Ireland. Parnell said the letter was a forgery, and Irish Members of Parliament claimed it was forged by the man through whom it was produced, Richard Pigott. Excitement grew, and a special commission of three judges was set up to enquire into the whole affair. Sir Charles Russell brusquely returned his general retainer from *The Times* and accepted instructions to act for Parnell.

On the Wednesday Pigott went into the witness-box. On the Thursday afternoon Russell began to cross-examine a reasonably cheerful and satisfied witness. Russell had a minute but deadly point. In one of the disputed letters the word 'hesitancy' was mis-spelt 'hesitency'. If Pigott spelt it this way, Russell was close to establishing Pigott as the forger. He opened his cross-examination.

RUSSELL : Mr Pigott, would you be good enough, with My Lords' permission, to write some words on that sheet of paper for me ? Would you like to sit down ?

PIGOTT : Oh no, thanks.

PRESIDENT : Well, but I think it is better that you should sit down. Here is a table upon which you can write in the ordinary way – the course you always pursue.

Pigott sat.

RUSSELL : Will you write the word 'livelihood' ?

Pigott wrote.

RUSSELL : Just leave a space. Will you write the word 'likelihood' ?

Pigott wrote.

RUSSELL : Will you write your own name ? Will you write the word 'proselytism', and finally – I think I will not trouble you at present any more – 'Patrick Egan' and 'P

Egan'?

Russell produced the names with formidable emphasis, and Pigott wrote, and prepared to hand back the paper.

RUSSELL (carelessly): There is one word I had forgotten, lower down, please, leaving spaces, write the word 'hesitancy'. (And then, as if this were the vital point) With a small 'h'.

Pigott wrote and picked up the blotting paper.

RUSSELL (sharply): Don't blot it, please.

The cross-examination proceeded all afternoon but it was never completed. By the next sitting of the court, Pigott had fled to Paris and had written a letter confessing to the forgery; and a fortnight later he shot himself. The awful hortation, the thunderous afternoon with Sir Charles, may have affected him, but Pigott's disaster struck at the start with the second 'e' he had inserted in 'hesitency'.

Everyone knows the scandal of the Oscar Wilde case in 1895 and, surprisingly enough, the moment of disaster came late in his cross-examination. Oscar Wilde began by enjoying himself.

CARSON: Do you adore him?
WILDE: No, but I have always liked him. I think it is a beautiful letter. It is a poem. I was not writing an ordinary letter. You might as well cross-examine me as to whether *King Lear* or a sonnet of Shakespeare was proper.
CARSON: Apart from art, Mr Wilde?
WILDE: I cannot answer apart from art.
CARSON: Suppose a man who was not an artist had written

this letter, would you say it was a proper letter?

WILDE: A man who was not an artist could not have written that letter.

CARSON: Why?

WILDE: Because nobody but an artist could write it. He certainly could not write the language unless he were a man of letters.

CARSON: I can suggest, for the sake of your reputation, that there is nothing very wonderful in this 'red rose-leaf lips of yours'?

WILDE: A great deal depends on the way it is read.

CARSON: 'Your slim gilt soul walks between passion and poetry' – is that a beautiful phrase?

WILDE: Not as you read it, Mr Carson. You read it very badly.

CARSON: I do not profess to be an artist; and when I hear you give evidence, I am glad I am not.

SIR EDWARD CLARKE: I don't think my friend should talk like that. (To the witness) Pray do not criticize my friend's reading again.

Sir Edward Clarke, honourable to the end as Wilde's counsel, found the whole sequence of cases involving his client increasingly distasteful. When he came to write his autobiography, published over twenty years later in 1918, he made no mention of Oscar Wilde, believing his tale unfitted for a book on offer to the general public.

Meanwhile the witness continued to flourish. Resolutely Carson pressed him towards the catastrophic admission, and the moment when he had gone too far for his own safety.

CARSON: Did you ever kiss him?

WILDE: Oh dear no. He was a peculiarly plain boy. He was, unfortunately, extremely ugly. I pitied him for it.

CARSON: Was that the reason why you did not kiss him?

WILDE: Oh, Mr Carson, you are pertinently insolent.

The art world of the 1890s, sharply divided between the followers of Whistler and those of Sickert, fell apart over a distinction between lithographs drawn on paper and lithographs drawn directly on the stone. These complex issues arose in a libel action brought by Joseph Penwell, the lithographer, against the *Saturday Review* and Sickert. George Moore, the esteemed writer and critic, came to give expert evidence.

'I can see him now,' wrote Max Beerbohm, 'placed there, more than ever wraith-like in the harsh, bleak light of the court. He kisses the book, he acknowledges that his name is George Moore, and that he is an art critic, and dimly he conveys an impression that he prefers lithographs drawn directly on the stone. Up rises the cross-examining counsel: "Now Mr Moore, I want you to explain what claim you have to be regarded as an expert in this matter." Silence reigned. Moore's gaze wandered to the judge, and then suddenly his tongue was loosened. "I know Degas . . ." he began ; whereat down sat the cross-examining counsel with an eloquent gesture to judge and jury ; the judge made a little gesture to the witness ; the ordeal was over.'

It is perhaps just as well that he did not survive to be pressed into service at the trial of *Lady Chatterley*. The shy expert witness often has a rotten time.

8. The Clubman to the Gamekeeper 1905 – 1960

Club expulsions have produced a most flourishing crop of legal disasters. All you need is an eccentric and litigious member, preferably rich, a committee of successful lawyers and busy men of affairs, and a fine emotional onslaught by the member on the values of the establishment. Both sides are aware of how desirable it is to build up a sequence of sententious letters for reading out in court, 'if it comes to that'.

Edward Martyn was the perfect candidate for the necessary member. Austere and stout, pious and rich, the last of an ancient Galway family which had preserved intact its Catholic faith, its castle and lands, he had achieved fame in Dublin as a patron of the arts, a playwright and a politician. He was a reactionary turned nationalist and was to become the first President of Sinn Fein. He had little interest in women or country life, and he preferred to devote himself to his causes from his club, the Kildare Street, in Dublin, where the secretary had provided him with a special high desk where he could stand to write. He was a Minor Institution of the club.

The club did not share his views. It was the social headquarters of the Protestant ascendancy in Ireland, of those eminent in service to the English Crown, and of the great landlords long settled on Irish estates.

The rumbling began during the Boer War when Martyn attacked the British in the Nationalist press. He received an anonymous club card: 'Had you not better resign your membership here before you are expelled?' But nothing came of it until after the war, when Edward VII decided to visit Ireland. Martyn at once wrote to the press declaring that Irishmen must not welcome the King but should turn their backs on him or cease to pretend any form of sympathy for self government in Ireland.

The committee fired their first shot. His letters to the press, wrote the club secretary, were 'derogatory to your position in society.' The committee desired to know 'whether you have any explanation to offer to them or reason to adduce why your conduct in writing such letters should not be referred to a General Meeting of the club as provided for under Rule XXV'. The letter was handed to him at the club. He went to stand at his desk.

'I beg to inform you', he wrote, 'that I consider my political opinions as expressed in my various published letters or other works in no wise derogatory to my station in society or to that of any other Irishman. I have no explanation to offer, and retract nothing, and await with perfect equanimity the decision of a general meeting of the club, should such be deemed advisable by the committee, to be called to decide a political matter in a club which is strictly non-political in its constitution.'

The committee struck back. The committee 'desire me to point out that suggestions that disrespect should be manifested to the Sovereign cannot be confounded with political opinions, and that the publication of such suggestions by a member of this club, cannot fail to be in the highest degree distasteful and offensive to your fellow members.'

Martyn knew very well the golden rule in rude correspondence: never leave a letter unanswered, or the court will wonder why. 'I believe I have a perfect right to show him disrespect, and I believe my action in so doing to be a political action, and consequently refuse to acknowledge the right of Kildare Street Club to dictate to me as to the propriety of such action.'

The committee, no cause for surprise, was thick with eminent lawyers. Nevertheless at their next weekly meeting, they decided to take counsel's opinion: the result: Rule XXV was stiffened up, at a general meeting of the club, by a majority of 152 votes to one, namely Martyn. All this took time and Martyn used it to counter-attack. He issued a manifesto to the press. 'The power of the Unionists as an ascendancy is fast going. They are, to those who really know them, but poor phantoms of what they once were ... a grotesque minority.' King Edward came and went. Gleefully Martyn discovered a political and conservative letter to the press written by a military member on club headed paper. 'You may remember,' he wrote blandly to the secretary, 'that we had some correspondence in which I was unjustly accused of breaking the above by-law ... I think it should be brought to the notice of the committee.' The committee had no choice but to get an apology from the member.

A month later the Sinn Fein journal carried the report of a speech by Martyn. The committee went into action. 'I am directed by the committee to ask,' wrote the secretary, 'if the speeches made by you on those occasions are correctly reported in that paper and more especially the following statement attributed to you, viz "The Irishman who enters the Army or Navy of England deserves to be flogged." I am further to add that in the event of your not denying the accuracy of these reports of your speeches, the committee will assume they are correctly reported in the paper.'

Martyn wrote at once to say that the reports were on the whole correct. 'Any explanation?' asked the secretary. 'No', wrote Martyn by return.

Battle was now joined. The letters were bundled up in chronological order. Eminent counsel inspected and amended the draft of a motion for Martyn's expulsion. Notice was given of a general meeting of the club. Martyn wrote to the secretary, asking for full notice of any motion to expel him. The committee sent off a letter to all members, that a ballot was to be held on the question of his expulsion. They gave him notice that a resolution was to be proposed at a special general meeting, declaring the opinion that his conduct had been injurious to the character and interests of the club. He was free to make a statement in writing to be posted in the morning-room before the ballot was taken.

Generals and admirals and hunt masters flooded the secretary's office with their annual subscriptions and the announcements that they would come to Dublin for the event. Among the flood was a letter from Martyn. Was it to be a proper meeting with discussion, or a bare ballot, the recording of votes? He enclosed his cheque for his subscription for the coming year.

The secretary consulted the most senior member, the Master of the Rolls. That afternoon, between 2 pm and 5 pm, many members recorded their votes: Martyn was declared unwanted and expelled.

At once he brought an action in the High Court in Dublin for wrongful expulsion. Presiding was the new Master of the Rolls, who had replaced in that office the secretary's adviser. For five days all Dublin had the pleasure of hearing its leading advocates perform; reading in measured terms the correspondence, calling evidence of Martyn's goings-on and the nature of the club.

The judgment of the learned Master of the Rolls fell like thunder. The club, under its Rules, had to have a proper meeting to expel a member. It had been argued that a ballot over an afternoon was a meeting. 'That view,' he said, 'is wrong. I decide that though the defendants, the committee of the club, acted in a manner which cannot be assailed by any right-minded person, though their integrity and honesty can never be called in question, yet the Rules, or the particular Rule under which they purported to act, did not give them the jurisdiction they assumed in this particular case, and the plaintiff, Mr Martyn, must succeed in his action.'

That night Martyn dined in the club. He was asked if he really proposed to go on using it. 'Of course I will,' he said, 'it's the only place in Dublin where I can get caviare.' Before, during and after the troubles, the civil war and the obtaining of Irish independence, Martyn was most often to be found in his club. He brought guests: priests and monks in particular, to out-face the generals. Occasionally he heard members

The committee did not try again to expel him . . .

swearing at him : promptly he would kneel in the smoking-room and produce a rosary, on which he recited prayers for their edification. He aged and had to be wheeled in a bath-chair Until his death in 1924 he remained a member. The committee did not try again to expel him. They failed to avoid disaster but knew that the best way to face it was to pay the lawyers' fees, and build up Edward Martyn as a Major Institution of the club.

Miss Gertie Millar was an Edwardian beauty, known throughout the kingdom from picture postcards and her stage appearances. She appeared nightly at the Gaiety, and one day in 1907 she appeared as a plaintiff in the court of Mr Justice Darling, supported by her manager, George Edwardes, and her husband, the famous song-writer, Lionel Monckton. She complained of libel. The defendants had bought photographs of her, extracted the heads, and substituted other bodies, so that Miss Millar appeared in the final products 'somewhat immodestly' as a nymph, in the act of bursting from an egg, and in a nightgown carrying a light. She had not sat for the pictures, or approved them, or been paid for them, and she was unamused. Mr Powell KC appeared for the defendants and he cross-examined her about the photograph in a nightgown.

POWELL : Will you agree that this is pretty?
MISS MILLAR : My objection to it is that it gives the impression I would be taken in that costume.
JUDGE : Supposing that there was a part on the stage in which it was necessary to dress like that, would you accept that part ?
MISS MILLAR : I have to earn my living, so I probably should.

POWELL: But you know that in a great many plays actresses have appeared in their nightgowns?

MISS MILLAR: No doubt.

POWELL: Would you think the worse of a lady who came on to the stage in her nightgown in the part of Lady Macbeth?

MISS MILLAR: Certainly not.

POWELL: You know that in *Othello* Desdemona is smothered in bed when she is in her nightgown?

MISS MILLAR: Yes.

POWELL: You don't suggest that ladies who have played Desdemona and have been photographed in that costume have been defamed thereby?

MISS MILLAR: No, I don't.

POWELL: Since these photographs, you are still well received at the theatre, are you not?

MISS MILLAR: Yes.

POWELL: Always a round of applause upon your entrance.

MISS MILLAR: I suppose the public likes my work.

POWELL: You have never been hissed as a result of these photographs?

MISS MILLAR: Certainly not.

POWELL: The publishers offered to have these photographs withdrawn?

MISS MILLAR: Yes, I know they did.

POWELL: Regret has been expressed?

MISS MILLAR: Yes, I know it has.

Then that disastrous moment for an advocate: the question too many.

POWELL: Then what more do you want?

MISS MILLAR: I want the public to know that I did not sit for them.

It should have been a disaster for Mr Powell. Miss Millar's answer was honest and summed up with feeling her motive for sueing. But it was Miss Millar who, unfairly I think, suffered the disaster. The jury gave a verdict for the defendants.

Leaving your papers behind in court is normally no disaster. A kindly usher will put them somewhere safe, and no one would dream of reading them. But the trial of Sir Roger Casement was an exception in many ways.

In April 1916 he had landed from a German submarine on the coast of County Kerry, and was soon picked up by the police and sent to London for trial for treason. Whether he hoped to lead the Easter revolt in Dublin, or stop it, or scout out the landings for a German invasion, was not clear.

Casement had been a distinguished civil servant who had accepted a knighthood in 1911 and devoted his retirement to the Irish nationalist cause and Home Rule. For Casement, a vigorous opponent of Carson and F.E. Smith, the pro-British lawyer politicians who championed the continuance of British rule, the war was a tiresome irrelevance. He went to Berlin, where for eighteen months he sought German help in freeing Ireland and Irish-born prisoners of war to join his Irish brigade. It was his work in Germany 'aiding and abetting the king's enemies' which was charged against him as the capital crime of high treason, and he was prosecuted by none other than F.E. Smith, now Attorney-General. The defence, put ably by Sergeant Sullivan of the Irish bar, was that Casement intended only to collect Irish volunteers to resist the Carson and Smith Ulster volunteers, and not to fight against England. The jury, to no one's great surprise, convicted, and it was then that the defendant delivered his speech. He robustly attacked the Attorney-General. 'The difference between us was that the Unionist champions chose a path they felt would lead to the Woolsack, while I went a road I knew must lead to the dock ... I am prouder to stand here today in the traitor's dock to answer this impeachment that to fill the place of my right honourable accusers.'

At this point the right honourable accuser, Sir F. E. Smith, was seen to smile and heard to murmur, 'Change places with him? Nothing doing.'

After the sentence of death came the agitation for a reprieve. Two jurors told Bernard Shaw that if they had heard Casement's speech before verdict they would have refused to convict. The Court of Appeal rejected his counsel's plea. The question of reprieve normally falls to the Home Secretary, but in this case the cabinet met more than once to discuss it; high politics were involved. The Irish party in the Commons wanted a reprieve: the British public was thought to want an execution. How would still neutral America react to the hanging of Casement?

The Government decided to apply that form of pressure favoured by politicians throughout history: the leak. The cabinet had Casement's diaries, which were irrelevant to the charge, but had been tendered before the trial to Casement's counsel in case he should wish to raise a defence of insanity. Counsel refused to read them, but members of the cabinet had. They gave a detailed description of his scandalous life as a homosexual, hitherto unsuspected. At dinner in Downing Street the Prime Minister offered to show them to the American ambassador, who replied that he had already seen them. 'Excellent,' said Mr Asquith, 'and you need not be particular about keeping them to yourself.'

The insults to the Attorney-General, the smear campaign, the wartime crisis, cannot have helped Casement, but his failure to look after his papers was the most probable direct cause of his execution. When he left the court after being sentenced he left his file behind. It was returned to him in prison, where he casually sealed it up and asked the governor to send it to his solicitors. The governor instead sent it to the Home Office for censoring, and there it was read, for the first time. One paper was a copy of an agreement dated December 1914 between Casement and the Germans whereby, in the event of the Germans being unable to transport his Irish brigade to Ireland, the brigade might be used in Egypt against the British. On another paper he had written : 'There is enough in these papers to hang me ten times over. If I had been thirty-three instead of fifty-three, the arms would have been landed, the code would not have been found, and I should have freed Ireland, or died fighting at the head of my men.'

There was no more talk of a reprieve.

The 'black book' trial took place towards the end of the Great War, in May 1918, when the outcome was still in doubt. Mr Pemberton-Billing, an Independent member of Parliament, spread tales that the British government was conducting peace negotiations with the Germans, and that the Germans had a secret weapon, namely a black book listing 47,000 debauched British perverts open to blackmail. At the same time the well known actress, Miss Maud Allan, undertook the role of Salome in a private production of Oscar Wilde's play, then banned from public performance in England. Mr Pemberton-Billing managed to get everything together in a few lines in his new paper, *The Vigilante*, under the eye-catching headline 'The Cult of the Clitoris'. He wrote :

'To be a member of Maud Allan's private performance in Oscar Wilde's *Salome* one has to apply to a Miss Valetta, of 9 Duke Street, Adelphi. If Scotland Yard were to seize the list of these members I have no doubt they would secure the names of several thousand of the first 47,000.'

Miss Allan prosecuted Mr Pemberton-Billing for criminal libel. Mr Pemberton-Billing, acting in person, proclaimed in writing that he was justified. 'The tragedy of *Salome*', he wrote, 'is a stage play by one Oscar Wilde, a moral pervert.' The play is 'an open representation of degenerated sexual lust,

116

sexual crime, and passions and an evil and mischievous travesty of a biblical story'. The Germans, he continued, have 'compiled a list of men and women of various social, political, financial and other positions in this country with a record of their alleged moral, sexual and other weaknesses'. A performance of *Salome* would, he claimed, bring them all out.

The case was tried by the celebrated wit, Mr Justice Darling, and a jury: nobody listened very much to anybody else, and it was pretty much disaster all round, particularly for poor Miss Allan when Mr Pemberton-Billing was acquitted of libel amid shrieks and roars from the public gallery. Before that point was reached there were some unsteady moments for the judge.

Mr Pemberton-Billing called as his first witness for the defence Mr Eileen Villiers Stuart, a rather pert young lady, soon after to be convicted of bigamy. She claimed to have seen and read the celebrated black book, and Mr Pemberton-Billing explored the titillating details with her.

JUDGE: If you undertake to conduct your own case, you ought to know you must conduct it according to the ordinary rules of evidence.

DEFENDANT: I know nothing about evidence, and I know nothing about law. I came to this court in the public interest to prove what I propose to prove.

JUDGE: Very well. Then you must prove it according to the ordinary rules of evidence.

DEFENDANT (to witness): Is Justice Darling's name in the book?

WITNESS: It is, and that book can be produced.

JUDGE: It can be produced?

WITNESS: It can be produced. It will have to be produced from Germany, and it can be, and it shall be. Mr Justice Darling, we have got to win this war, and while you sit there we will never win it. My men are fighting, other people's men are fighting –

DEFENDANT: Is Mrs Asquith's name in the book?

WITNESS: It is.

117

DEFENDANT: Is Mr Asquith's name in the book?

WITNESS: It is.

DEFENDANT: Is Lord Haldane's name in the book?

WITNESS: It is in the book.

JUDGE: Leave the box.

WITNESS: You dare not hear me.

JUDGE (to defendant): ... I have not the *least* objection to your having asked the one regarding myself, but I am determined to protect other people who are absent.

If Mrs Villiers Stuart was a trying witness for the judge to control, she was nothing compared to Lord Alfred Douglas, the former friend of Oscar Wilde, who came to give evidence for Mr Pemberton-Billing on his views on *Salome*. He was cross-examined by counsel for Miss Allan.

COUNSEL: The letter begins 'My own Boy'. Then it says, 'Your sonnet is quite lovely, and it is a marvel that those red rose-leaf lips of yours should have been made no less for music of song than for madness of kisses. Your slim gilt soul walks between passion and poetry ... Always, with undying love, yours, Oscar.' Is that a sample?

WITNESS: Yes, it is. It is just exactly what I said it was. It is a rotten sodomitically inclined letter written by a diabolical scoundrel to a wretched silly youth. You ought to be ashamed to bring it out here.

JUDGE: You are not here to comment on counsel.

WITNESS: I shall answer the questions as I please. I came here to give my evidence. You bullied me at the last trial; I shall not be bullied and brow-beaten by you again. You deliberately lost me my case in the last trial. I shall answer the questions as I choose, and not as you choose. I shall speak the truth.

JUDGE: You shall not make rude speeches, or you will be removed from the court.

WITNESS: Let me be removed from the court; I did not want to come here to be cross-examined to help out this gang of scoundrels they have at the back of them. If you are taking down a note of anything I said, take down all I have said.

Some laughter in court.

JUDGE: Anyone who interferes in this case in a disorderly manner, I do not care who it is, will be at once expelled from the court.
DEFENDANT: May we laugh at *your* jokes, My Lord?
JUDGE: No you may not.

Lord Alfred was not expelled from the court during his evidence but during the judge's summing-up to the jury. The judge had hinted that Lord Alfred had had a share in inspiring or writing *Salome*. Lord Alfred departed with a fine line. 'You have no right to say that I wrote it,' he bleated. 'You lie. You are a liar. If you say it outside the court I will prosecute you.'

It was an effective exit, but even this he spoiled. He reappeared a few minutes later to ask if he could collect his hat.

Mr Horatio Bottomley, the editor of *John Bull*, was a national figure who had talked himself out of trouble time and time again. In 1922 he was charged with fraudulently converting to his own use the funds of a club he had started in connection with the Government's Victory Loan. His case was hopeless, but he addressed the jury with spirit. 'You have got to find that I had the intention to steal the money of poor devils, such as ex-soldiers, who subscribed to the club. You have got to find that Horatio Bottomley, editor of *John Bull*, Member of Parliament, the man who wrote and spoke throughout the war with the sole object of inspiring the troops and keeping up the morale of the country, who went out to the front to do his best to cheer the lads – you have got to find that that man intended to steal their money. God forbid! God forbid.'

119

Lord Alfred Douglas, to Mr Justice Darling : You are a liar. If you say it outside the court I will prosecute you.

He was convicted and sentenced to seven years' imprisonment, the judge commenting on his 'callous effrontery'.

BOTTOMLEY: I was under the impression that it is put to an accused person, 'Have you anything to say before sentence is passed'?

JUDGE: It is not customary in the case of a misdemeanour like fraudulent conversion.

BOTTOMLEY: Had it been so, My Lord, I would have had something rather offensive to say about your summing-up.

In November 1930, the love-life of Mr A. A. Rouse was complicated and distressing to him, and he decided to disappear without trace. He picked up a vagrant in his car, drove him towards Northampton, pulled the car off the road, strangled the vagrant, set fire to the car and fled. Mr Rouse was both unlucky and an incompetent liar, and the police did not assume the dead man was he. He was caught and tried for murder. His defence was simple: he had given a lift to an unknown man, he had got out to urinate, and had asked him while he was away to fill the petrol tank from a can. The man, half asleep, had said something to him about smoking and must have set light to the car, and when Mr Rouse returned, the car was a mass of flames.

The case turned on technical evidence. Why was the carburettor top found to be loose? Why was the petrol union brass nut found to be loose? The evidence called for the prosecution was very damaging to Mr Rouse. Had he deliberately loosened the parts to spread petrol around and then set the car alight? Or did the parts loosen themselves when the car caught fire and reached a high temperature?

Mr Isaacs came forward to give expert evidence for the

defence. He was the managing director of a manufacturing company specializing in the heat treatment of metals. He asserted that the nut on the union joint invariably loosened of its own accord when an intense fire raged near it. He had come forward to give evidence as a public duty when he read of the case in the papers. He was a wholly independent witness, his evidence was formidable, and what was Mr Norman Birkett, counsel for the prosecution, going to do about it? He rose to cross-examine.

BIRKETT: What is the coefficient of the expansion of brass?
ISAACS: I am afraid I cannot answer that question off-hand.
BIRKETT: If you do not know, say so. What do I mean by the term?
ISAACS: You want to know what is the expansion of the metal under heat?
BIRKETT: I asked you what is the coefficient of the expansion of brass? You do not know?
ISAACS: No, not put that way.

The witness was demolished. Mr Rouse was hanged, and the next day the *Daily Sketch* published his confession: he had both loosened the petrol union joint and taken the top off the carburettor. The coefficient of the expansion of brass is 0.0000189.

When in later years Norman Birkett was asked what he would have done if Mr Isaacs had known the answer, he said he would have promptly asked him the coefficient of the expansion of copper, and then of aluminium. If the witness had known the answers, he would have moved on to something else with a suggestion that it was of no importance.

Norman Birkett was not the only grand master during the

1930s of the simple but shattering question. Here is Patrick Hastings repeating the same question until the witness is seen as a hopeless prevaricator. He is cross-examining a defendant in an action for slander where the defendant had hinted to the plaintiff's employers at the BBC that the plaintiff was mad.

HASTINGS: If a man spoke to you about a friend and interspersed his observations by tapping his forehead and saying, 'You know,' what would you understand that to mean?

DEFENDANT: I saw a film a few days ago, where the tapping of the head –

HASTINGS: Did you hear my question? I am not interested in your film experience. What would you understand him to mean?

DEFENDANT: I said that that is the conventional sign –

HASTINGS: I will ask you once more. What would you understand him to mean?

DEFENDANT: To mean that he was lacking in intelligence.

HASTINGS: That he was out of his mind?

DEFENDANT: Not necessarily.

HASTINGS: You realize, do you not, that at some time your evidence may have to be criticized before the jury? Just think once more. What would you understand him to mean?

DEFENDANT: That he was out of his mind.

The defendant had to pay heavy damages. On the brighter side, the Prime Minister ordered an enquiry into the possible gullibility of the BBC.

Here are three sentences which evoked instant laughter from the jury and eventual disaster for the prosecution. The alleged obscenity of D. H. Lawrence's *Lady Chatterley's Lover* was on trial, whether the dissemination of two hundred thousand copies at three shillings and sixpence apiece would tend to deprave and corrupt the public.

In October 1960 the trial opened at the Old Bailey, with an empty dock, the defendant being a limited company, Penguin Books Limited, a packed press box and a queue of eminent witnesses. Counsel opened the case for the Crown and for a moment addressed the jury – nine men and three women – as if they were heads of Victorian households. Echoing the Agar-Ellis case, Mr Griffith-Jones began:

'You may think that one of the ways in which you can test this book, and test it from the most liberal outlook, is to ask yourselves the question, when you have read it through, would you approve of your young sons, young daughters – because girls can read as well as boys – reading this book? Is it a book that you would have lying around in your own house? Is it a book that you would even wish your wife or your servants to read?'

No, he might have added, the boys and girls, the wives and servants should stick to *Alice in Wonderland*. There they would have found the proper tail-piece to a book of legal disasters:

Fury said to a mouse, That
he met in the
house, 'Let
us both go
to law: I will
prosecute *you*.
Come, I'll take
no denial: We
must have
the trial;
For really
this morning
I've nothing
to do.'
Said the
mouse to
the cur,
'Such a
trial, dear
sir, With
no jury
or judge,
would be
wasting our
breath.'
'I'll be
judge,
I'll be
jury,'
said
cun-
ning
old
Fury:
I'll
try
the
whole
cause,
And
con-
demn
you to
death.'

Very Select List of Books

(excluding Pope, Boswell, Macaulay, Archbold,
1878 Chancery 49 and 1883 Chancery 317)

The dates below refer to the editions consulted, not to the first
editions.

Anon. *Remarkable Trials* (including the Hammersmith Ghost)
(London, 1804)

Ballantine, Mr Serjeant *Some Experiences of a Barrister's
Life* (London, 1883)

(1) Beerbohm, Max *Mainly on the Air* (London, 1957)

(1) Beerbohm, Max *Yet Again* (London, 1923)

Bentley, G.E. Jr *Blake Records* (Oxford, 1969)

(1) Bewley, Christina *Muir of Huntershill* (Oxford, 1981)

Birkett, Sir Norman (ed) *The Newgate Calendar* (London,
1951)

(1) Bishop, Marchand *Blake's Hayley* (London, 1951)

Blackstone, Sir William *Commentaries on the Laws of
England* (London, 1793)

Bowen-Rowlands *Seventy-Two Years at the Bar* (London,
1924)

Bronowski, J. *William Blake and the Age of Revolution*
(London, 1972)

Bruce, Ian *The Nun of Lebanon* (London, 1951)

Campbell, Lord *Lives of the Chancellors* (London, 1856–7)

Campbell, Lord *Lives of the Chief Justices* (London, 1858)

Clarke, Rt. Hon. Sir Edward *The Story of My Life*
(London, 1918)

Cockburn, Lord *Memories of His Time* (Edinburgh and
London, 1910)

Foote, J.H., Q.C. *Pie-Powder* (London, 1911)

Gardiner, G., K.C. and Curtis-Raleigh, N. *The Judicial*

Attitude to Penal Reform (London, 1949)

Gilchrist, Alexander *The Life of William Blake* (London, 1863)

Gwynn, Denis *Edward Martyn and the Irish Revival* (London, 1930)

Hale, Sir Matthew *Pleas of the Crown* (London, 1778)

Hardcastle, Mrs (ed) *Life of Lord Campbell* (London, 1881)

Harris, R., K.C. *The Reminiscences of Sir Henry Hawkins* (London, n.d.)

Hawkes, C.P. *Bench and Bar in the Saddle* (London, 1932)

(1) Healy, Maurice *The Old Munster Circuit* (London, 1939)

Herzen, Alexander (trans. Garnett, C.) *My Past and Thoughts* (London, 1968)

Humphreys, Travers *Criminal Days* (London, 1946)

Hyde, H. Montgomery *Roger Casement* (London, 1964)

Hyde, H. Montgomery *Norman Birkett* (London, 1964)

Hyde, H. Montgomery *Their Good Names* (London, 1970)

Hyde, H. Montgomery (ed) *The Trials of Oscar Wilde* (London, 1948)

Kettle, Michael *Salome's Last Veil* (London, 1977)

Keynes, Sir Geoffrey *The Letters of William Blake* (Oxford, 1980)

Knott, G.H. (ed) *The Trial of Roger Casement* (Edinburgh and London, 1917)

Lustgarten, Edgar *The Judges and the Judged* (London, 1961)

Mackinnon, Sir F.D. *On Circuit* (Cambridge, 1940)

Marjoribanks, E. *The Life of Sir Edward Marshall-Hall* (London, 1929)

Mavor, Elizabeth *The Virgin Mistress* (London, 1964)

Megarry, R.E. *Miscellany-at-Law* (London, 1955)

Melville, Lewis *The Trial of the Duchess of Kingston* (London, 1927)

(1) Moore, George *Hail and Farewell* (London, 1911)

Nash, T.A. *Life of Lord Chancellor Westbury* (London, 1888)

Normanton, Helena (ed) *The Trial of Alfred Arthur Rouse* (Edinburgh and London, 1931)

O'Brien, R. Barry *The Life of Lord Russell of Kilrowen* (London, n.d.)

(2) Peacock, T. L. *The Novels* (ed Garnett, D.) (London, 1977)

Pearson, Hesketh *Gilbert and Sullivan* (London, 1935)

Rolph, C.H. (ed) *The Trial of Lady Chatterley* (Privately printed 1961)

Roughead, William *The Riddle of the Rathvens and Other Studies* (Edinburgh and London, 1936)

Roughead, William (ed) *The Trial of Deacon Brodie* (London, 1907)

Roughead, William *Twelve Scots Trials* (Edinburgh and London, 1913)

Sellar, W.C. and Yeatman, R.J. *1066 and All That* (London, 1937)

Stephen, H.L. (ed) *State Trials Political and Social* (London, 1899)

(2) Torr, Cecil *Small Talk at Wreyland* (Oxford, 1981)

Twiss, H., K.C. *The Public and Private Life of Lord Chancellor Eldon* (London, 1844)

Watt, Francis *Terrors of the Law* (London, 1902)

Whistler, J. McNeill *The Baronet and the Butterfly* (Paris, 1898)

(1) White, T.H. *The Age of Scandal* (London, 1950)

Williams, Montagu, Q.C. *Leaves of a Life* (London, 1890)

Wilson, Mara *The Life of William Blake* (London, 1958)

(2) Wu Cheng-En (trans. Waley, A.) *Monkey* (London, 1942)

Notes:
(1) This book should be kept permanently in print, bought, read and cherished.
(2) This book is completely irrelevant, save that note (1) applies just the same.